Footprints in the Water

by

Peter Hay

Copyright © 2015 Peter Hay
All Rights Reserved

ISBN: 978-1-329-68521-5

Table of Contents

Acknowledgements	-
Introduction	6
The River of God	10
The Victory of God	20
The Pursuit of God	29
The Will of God	38
The Cross of Christ	49
The Spirit of Prayer	59
The Call to Wait	70
The Grace of God	79
The End of Self	88
The Love of God	99
Conclusion	114

Acknowledgements

My greatest influence has been my wife Gwyn, a true and fragrant saint who has a love for God and all His children that has amazed all who know her. It has been my privilege to know her and to be married to her for over 40 years. Through her I have been challenged in my own walk with God almost daily.

I would also like to thank the congregations I have pastored over the last 33 years. I have learned the hard way that God is far more interested in our spiritual growth and development than He is in our ministry. Indeed He sometimes puts men in ministry because it forces them to face their character flaws and weaknesses. All the churches I have pastored have essentially put up with the ongoing crucible of God's work in me. I have contributed very little while their input into my life has been generous and kind and patient. May God bless them with better men than I.

Thanks to Keith Walker for providing the impetus and means to finish the process of publishing this book.

Peter Hay

Introduction

> "This soft quiet light which is simple and pure and full of love is St. John of the Cross's 'pure faith' and 'hidden faith': 'the dark and loving knowledge which is faith' (ibid.). If we let it, this light will lead us by its most secret way following 'footprints on the water'.[1]

When Peter stepped out of the boat onto the water he stepped out into that realm beyond human limitation. The laws of physics were not just defied; they were bypassed. It has been fashionable in the past few years to preach sermons, often with the theme "step out of your boat" and the exhortation to take a chance on God, but they invariably miss the true point of the story. Faith has little to do with boldness and even less with "take a chance". Faith is not about us but about God. Apart from his Lord Peter could never have walked on water that day and it is almost certain that he never did again. Neither do we have any record of his fellow disciples who witnessed this miracle following his example.

Were such a miracle to happen in our day I have no doubt seminars and conferences would immediately follow with the purpose of teaching the principles of walking on water. It is a modern preoccupation with manifestations and reproducing them that causes us to miss the overarching focus of Christ's incarnation and work of salvation. Everything Jesus did was to bring us into a restored relationship with his Heavenly Father. The walking on water miracle was never about the miracle but always about trusting faith and through it knowing God. Instead of asking how I too can walk on water we must ask what does this story teach me about knowing God?

---

[1] Georges Lefebvre, Simplicity <u>The Heart of Prayer</u> (New York: Paulist Press, 1975), 16.

This is the purpose of this book and Peter's experience portrays some of the fundamental truths that underlie any endeavor to understand our journey to the knowledge of God. Paul declared that he wanted "to know Christ and the power of his resurrection and the fellowship of sharing in his suffering becoming like him in his death." (Peter 3:10) Though called to a world changing apostolic ministry Paul's first objective was "the prize of the high calling", to know Him – and in knowing Him to better make Him known.

How do we 'pursue' God as A.W. Tozer expressed it so powerfully? How can we know the infinite eternal God of the universe in our finite bodies and a fallen world? Jesus answered that he is "the way, the truth and the life." (John 14:6) And so when Peter heard the answer to his question "Is it you Lord?" - "Come!" he was able to step out onto the water and go to the One who is the way. Only through Christ the Lord could he walk on the water and only through Him can we know God. In Him alone is the truth and the life. There is no one else to whom we can go to. Thus we must both listen to Jesus and observe everything that He was and that He did if we wish to know God. His words, "He who has seen me has seen the Father" and His descriptions of His relationship with the Father are meant to guide us in our own walk with God. This is why Jesus called His disciples to take up the cross and follow Him! The purpose of discipleship is to not just imitate the teacher but to become like Him. Paul said follow me in so much as I follow Christ.

In the succeeding chapters it is our purpose to direct you in the path of following Christ. Scripture is always our road map in this journey but scripture can be used to suit our own purposes rather than those intended by God. Even a cursory look at the life of Christ should tell us that following Him means suffering, rejection, serving and self-denial. Anyone who teaches this will most likely receive a negative response. It actually appears that a true call to a deeper life with God is currently being trumped by a call to prosperity and glory that looks suspiciously consistent with the values of modern Western culture. Thus what follows is neither popular nor easily accessible. Our modern minds demand clear step-by-step principles and visibly achievable ends. This isn't just difficult; it is impossible for those who aspire to a life of increasing intimacy with God. Peter illustrates the loss of any certainty or safety. He has no precedent and after a lifetime of working on the water he knew without a doubt that what he was about to do was impossible. But we see that as long as he kept his eyes on Jesus he succeeded. He faltered only as his attention was drawn away by the wind and the waves. There are several powerful lessons of faith in this miracle but this is the single most important one. A second is the lesson of footprints. Water is always moving. Whoever would walk on water will always be walking where no one else has ever walked before. Every step in our journey to knowing God is a unique walk of faith sustained by one connection to the Kingdom – the King. Therefore there are no footsteps in the water that we can follow. To write a book that clearly outlines the path to knowing God is a challenge beyond any one person's understanding and the result will necessarily lack specifics and the kind of clarity modern Christians demand.

When Jesus called Peter to come, only faith in the Lord responding in obedience could take him out of that boat. Anyone who asks for more certainty before acting will never reach out and touch God nor will he know the supernatural experience of the manifest presence of God. Habakkuk wrote the words echoed by the writer to the Hebrews. – The righteous will live by faith. (Heb. 10:38) The walk towards intimacy with God is a faith walk.

What we will see as the following chapters unfold is that the greatest obstacle to stepping out of the boat in faith is what Paul called "the old man" – the self-life. Self wants proof, evidence before acting in order to retain control of everything we do. To step out in faith in God is to lose all control. Fear keeps us bound and thus from entering into the deeper life. Christ has won a complete victory for us. Our inheritance – all the fullness of Christ awaits every believer. Few experience this fullness in this world and our purpose in this book is to convince the reader that there is much more, even infinitely more available to the children of God. Indeed, our Father in Heaven longs for us to enter into all he has for us if we will only come. Let us step out of the boat together and take that first step. The river of God awaits and the rivers of living water can flow from your inner being as our Lord promised.

Chapter One
The River Of God

There is a scene at the end of the movie "The Lion, The Witch and the Wardrobe" that speaks to the appeal of the whole series of books written by C.S. Lewis. Lucy is sitting in front of the wardrobe by which she and her siblings passed into Narnia. The professor comes in, stands quietly for a moment, and then says: "You won't get back in that way again!" In that moment Lucy embodies the desire we all have to enter into a supernatural realm where we function with authority, power and concrete effectiveness as followers of Christ. Instead we find ourselves on the outside looking in or remembering a time, likely when we were new converts, when everything was new, exciting and very much alive.

After all Jesus promised that his disciples would do greater works (John 14:12) and that out or our bellies would flow "rivers of living water." (John 7:37-39) At times it seems these very promises mock us. One old hymn declares: "Mercy drops 'round us are falling, but for the showers we plead." Instead of rivers of living water we run around in a poor rainfall trying to satisfy our thirst by catching the occasional drop on our tongues. If there is one scripture that many of us have found we easily identify with it is: "As the deer pants for the streams of water so my soul longs for you" (Psalm 42:1).

The day we were born into the Kingdom of God, the most marvelous miracle imaginable took place. We became "new creatures in Christ" (2 Corinthians 5:17) by virtue of the regenerating work of the Holy Spirit. In that moment we moved from death to life. Once we were dead in our sins, and because of this it is hard for us to comprehend the amazing change that has taken place. Once alive in Christ it seems to be the most natural thing in the world. And it is. We become, or are becoming, what we were always meant to be. It is death that is unnatural. At the instant of spiritual conception the Holy Spirit began to dwell in an inner temple in the center of our being. This temple has always been present and it explains why man is a worshipper of gods. As God designed us to be worshippers the breaking of our relationship with Him through Adam and Eve left us with an empty temple and thus a longing to fill it with God however we choose to conceive of Him. This instinct remains with us even into the so-called post-modern era.

To understand how we respond to this we need only look at Adam and Eve in Genesis 3:8-13. Having sinned they felt compelled to physically hide from God and when confronted with their sin they, in turn, attempted to pass the blame; from Adam to Eve, from Eve to the serpent. If anyone should have known the impossibility of hiding from God and thus from the truth it would have been Adam and Eve. Ever since men have reacted in precisely the same manner, never deceiving God, but in actuality deceiving themselves. With the need to worship as fundamental as the need to nourish our bodies the only way man can satisfy this inborn desire is to create false gods. Ultimately as Paul describes it in Romans man willfully "exchange(s) the glory of the immortal God for images made to look like mortal man and birds and animals and reptiles." (Romans 1:23) The prophets, Isaiah, Jeremiah, and Ezekiel all ridiculed this practice, mocking the man who went out and cut down a tree, carved it into an idol and then used the rest of the wood in a fire to cook his dinner. It seems irrational but to those "dead in sin" they are actually responding to the creation driven DNA in their souls. A hunger, a thirst for God is inescapable even though it may be radically twisted or even perverted into things like child sacrifice or temple prostitution.

One might argue that we post-moderns no longer worship idols. By this we mean that we don't have wooden or metal statues to which we offer sacrifices anymore. However, evidence of idolatry is not at all difficult to see in 21st century life and culture. The screaming crowds of worshippers at a music concert or a Justin Bieber appearance attest to this. The objects of worship have changed from dumb blocks of wood but the practice of worship has never been more in vogue. We worship money, fame, power and sex, and, most particularly, those who have been able to succeed in gathering all of them to themselves. One could add "success" to this modern pantheon. The new commandments are greed, materialism, sensuality, control and selfishness, although it might be argued there is nothing at all new about them. There is indeed nothing new under the sun except, perhaps, old sins in new disguises. We have been and always will be driven to worship.

I ask you to imagine a temple deep within, a place designed originally to be alive with the presence of the infinite eternal God, a place of communion with Him. I say "imagine" but I have no doubt that such a place exists. In fact, the apostle Paul testifies to it in Corinthians. "Don't you know that you are God's temple and that God's Spirit lives in you?" (1 Corinthians 3:16) The reality of this indwelling presence of Christ has been sorely neglected in what has been an age of rationalism that emphasizes doctrine over experiencing the manifest presence of God. An unfortunate consequence of the pendulum swing back to *sola scriptura* in the reformation era was a tendency to be suspicious of what was then deemed mysticism or "enthusiasm." Sometimes the pendulum doesn't stop and historic truth is lost in a reactionary rush to a new/old recovery of faith. The other wing of the reformation phoenix was *sola fide*. Faith alone came to be narrowly interpreted as faith in the truth of scripture without the necessity of spiritual experience.

The great reality of "Christ in us the hope of glory" is lost to many who are doctrinally sound but have little or no knowledge of the privilege Christ has won for them as living temples of God. Their response to Paul's question might be "No, I didn't know that" or "Yes, I know it to be doctrinally true but what does it mean to me personally?" My answer, I think Paul's would be the same, is that it is everything.

Christ did not go to the cross to save us from hell. He did it to restore a living, loving communion between us and the Father. A temple, is by biblical definition to be a place of worship, and, if all is in order, of the presence of God.
Moses was instructed by God on the holy mountain to build the tabernacle exactly as he was told:

> "See to it that you make everything according to the pattern shown you on the mountain." (Exodus 2:5:40, Hebrews 5)

Exodus 39:30 affirms that Moses inspected the work and that is exactly what was done: "So all the work on the tabernacle, the tent of meeting, was completed. The Israelites did everything just as the Lord commanded Moses." (39:32) The result was immediate and spectacular. "The glory of the Lord covered the tent of meeting, and the glory of the Lord filled the tabernacle. Moses could not enter the tent of meeting because the cloud had settled upon it, and the glory of the Lord filled the tabernacle." (40:34, 35) This is an extraordinary statement. The glory so filled the tabernacle that even Moses who spent 40 days on the fiery mountain with God could not enter.

The writer to the Hebrews in referring to this amazing manifestation of the presence of God declared:

> "But the ministry Jesus has received is superior to theirs as the covenant whom He is mediator is superior to the old one, and it is founded on better promises." (Heb. 8:6)

God blessed this "copy and shadow" of the true tabernacle even though it was only a representation of the real one to come in and through the work of Christ. How then could we who are now the temple, the dwelling place of God expect so much less in experience of the glory of God?

This same experience was repeated when Solomon built the first temple. David gave the plans to Solomon in 1 Chronicles 28:9 affirming "All this I have in writing from the hand of the Lord upon me, and He gave me understanding in all the depths of the plan." He charged Solomon to follow the plan exactly and he did with the same spectacular result. "Then the temple of the Lord was filled with a cloud, and the priests could not perform their service because of the cloud, for the glory of the Lord filled the temple of God." (2 Chronicles 5:13-14) Paul tells us "everything that was written in the past was written to teach us…" (Romans 15:4) What other conclusion could we draw from the temple stories but that God makes temples to be His dwelling place. "Do you not know that you are the temple of God and that God's Spirit dwells in you?" Shouldn't our experience of this be "better" according to the writer to the Hebrews? When Jesus cried "It is finished!" and the veil blocking access to the Holy Place was torn from top to bottom were we not to understand that from that moment we had access to the presence of God without limit?

> "Therefore, brothers, since we have confidence to enter the most holy place by the blood of Jesus, by a new and living way opened for us through the curtain, that is, His body...let us draw near to God with a sincere heart in full assurance of faith, ..." (Heb. 10:19-22)

The blood of Christ has removed every obstacle between us and the presence of God. Indeed we are enjoined by Paul to come "boldly" to the throne of grace. Nothing hinders but our own reluctance to enter in. The reasons for this will be addressed in subsequent chapters but we must deal with the first and most important one – ignorance!

Psalm 46:4 states, "There is a river whose streams make glad the city of God, the holy place where the most high dwells. The psalmist counsels men to find refuge in the shadow of (the Lord's) wings, to feast on the abundance of His house and drink from (His) river of delights. For with (Him) is the fountain of life. (Psalm 36:7-9) It is commonly understood that Jerusalem is a type of the heavenly city that will come down out of heaven. (Rev. 21:1-2) Hence its designation, the new Jerusalem. As in the old city the new will have a temple, only in the new it is the bride that will be the temple, the dwelling place of God. But Paul's very pointed question affirms that already God dwells in each and every believer and thus we have become temples of the Spirit of God. If we grasp the "shadow and copy" message of the writer of Hebrews, what is true about the old temple is fulfilled in the new.

In Ezekiel the prophet describes a type of the heavenly temple from chapters 40-48. In chapter 47 he describes a river coming from under the threshold of the temple. This river brings life where it flows and along its banks are fruit trees whose leaves are for healing. Rev. 22 speaks of this same river of life that "flows from the throne of God." (1)   This is why Jesus declared to those who would become the temples of the Spirit of God that "rivers of living water would flow from (their) bellies. The Lord Himself knew that once he sent the Holy Spirit to take his place that the true temples of God would be filled once again and that men and women would begin to function as God created them to be.

It is this expectation of the indwelling glory and presence of God that so many Christians are ignorant of. We were made to bring forth rivers of living water that would bring life and healing to the world around us, just as Jesus did when he walked on this earth. In giving us the task of the Great Commission he also bestowed on us the same communion and relationship with the Father that sustained Him in His calling.

> "My prayer is not for them alone. I pray also for those who will believe in me through their message, that all of them may be one, Father, just as you are in me and I am in you. May they also be in us so that the world may believe that you have sent me. I have given them the glory that you gave me, that they may be one as we are one: I in them and you in me. May they be brought to complete unity to let the world know that you sent me and have loved them even as you have loved me." (John 17:20-23)

The idea that we get saved and then wait for a heavenly reward while we hold on to a creedal confession is simply not biblical. Our temples are to be places of meeting with God and sources of living water. Of course if you don't know this you won't expect it. These are not just doctrines they are the words, the promises of the living God. You are a temple and all you need to do to understand what is supposed to happen in a temple is read your bible. See Moses' tabernacle, Solomon's temple, Ezekiel and the New Jerusalem in Revelations. What was historically and what will be prophetically is the key to understanding who you are now. Yes the glory of God did not stay on the first earthly copies, because as the writer to the Hebrews declares:

> "The law is only a shadow of the good things…" (Heb. 10:1-3)

Christ made a once for all sacrifice and declared, "It is finished." Peter declares:

> Praise be the to God and Father of our Lord Jesus Christ, who has blessed us in the heavenly realms with every spiritual blessing in Christ. (Eph. 1:3)

The father has blessed us with <u>every</u> spiritual blessing in Christ. There are those who would bring forth the already/not yet argument suggesting that the Father has deferred the blessing of an intimate relationship with Him until Heaven. It is even seen as virtuous for us to simply believe the promise and wait for Heaven in faith. This is a very wrong apprehension of faith. Hebrews 11:1 is often misunderstood and misquoted. Faith isn't about believing in something that is unreal. It is believing in something that is really there even though we don't see it. God's love is as real as is His presence. Believing by faith in what we do not see actively allows us to access and participate in it just as Abraham did. He became the friend of God because he believed God and it was accounted to Him for righteousness.

Why would Paul say we are already temples of God and that His Spirit dwells in us if He did not mean we should expect to function as a temple now? A temple in scripture was the designated place of the presence of God. As we have already shown from the Old Testament records, that presence was expected to be real and active. Should we expect any less?

Isaiah summons us to the banqueting table of the Lord and the River of Life (Isaiah 55:1-2), as did the psalmist in the 23rd Psalm.

> The Lord is my shepherd, I shall not be in want, He makes me lie down in green pastures, he leads me beside quiet waters, He restores my soul. He guides me in paths of righteousness even though I walk through the valley of the shadow of death. I will fear no evil, for you are with me; your rod and your staff, they comfort me. You prepare a table before me in the presence of my enemies. You anoint my head with oil; my cup overflows. Surely goodness and love will follow me all the days of my life, and I will dwell in the house of the Lord forever. Psalm 23

Conclusions:

1. As new creations in Christ we are now temples of the living God.

2. As temples we are made to be the dwelling place of the presence of God.
3. As royal priests (1 Peter 1) we are called to worship in the presence of God and draw our very life from his dwelling place.
4. Because He dwells within according to the promise of the Lord Jesus "rivers of living water" (John 7:37-39) should come forth from this temple for the benefit of all whom we come into contact with.

Chapter Two
The Victory of God

Having established that the presence of God is a blessed gift and privilege for every believer it is necessary to unwrap the gift fully and discover all that it means to us. Because we are physical beings in a finite reality we tend to conform our understanding of God to our own limitations. But the Lord declares otherwise:

> "For my thoughts are not your thoughts, neither are your ways my ways," declares the Lord, "For as the heaven's are higher than the earth, so are my ways higher than your ways and my thoughts than your thoughts." (Isaiah 55:8-9)

We are far more comfortable with a God who is down to "earth", one of our own making, one we can understand, or one who is far away up in Heaven. This is why we pray "up" to God in Heaven or sing our worship songs with the implied intent of bringing Him down to our services. These are human constructions designed to give our actions meaning and to empower us in our interaction with God. But His ways are not at all like ours. We cannot logically wrap our minds around the indwelling, personal presence of God and the infinite eternal omnipresent God in scripture. How can He be omniscient and omnipresent and yet contain Himself within my inner temple? How does the infinite interact with the finite? Because we cannot grasp this we develop religious practices and mindsets that are based on making us secure and comfortable with questions that have no answers. Accepting His word by faith is what God has called us to. But faith isn't comfortable. It is stepping out of the boat into the ways of God that are not, in any way, like ours.

Walking on water defies everything we know about physics. Walking in the Spirit is walking in a realm we have no experience or understanding of. The Spirit moves like the wind:

> "The wind blows wherever it pleases. You hear its sound, but you cannot tell where it comes from or where it is going, so it is with everyone born of the spirit." (John 3:8)

How then shall we begin to live a life of which we have absolutely no understanding. In reply to Thomas's question along the same line Jesus gave a full and complete answer to every believer who wishes to live in victory.

> "…How can we know the way?" Jesus answers, "I am the way the truth and the life." (John 14:5b, 6a)

It is the all-sufficiency of the person and work of Christ that has given us a total victory, one that few experience and fewer still know of.

In Psalm 46 the Psalmist presents a wonderful picture of victory in God. He speaks of the city of God and within her is the dwelling place of God "The Holy Place". We have already discussed this in chapter one. This speaks prophetically of the fulfilment in the Church in Revelations. The Psalmist is telling us what it means to live in the dwelling place of God.

1. God is our refuge and strength, an <u>ever-present</u> help in trouble. (vs. 1)
2. God is within her, she will <u>not fall</u>. (vs. 5)
3. God will <u>help her</u>… (vs. 5)

4. The Lord almighty <u>is with us</u>; the God of Jacob is our fortress. (vs. 7)
5. Be still and know that I am God. (vs. 10)

The picture is one of complete victory because God is present in the midst of his people. Yet we know that even though the kingdom of Israel walked in this victory in David's lifetime, it did not last because of the unfaithfulness of the Israelites. One of the most tragic moments in Israel's history is Ezekiel's description of the departure of the presence of God from His temple in the tenth chapter. This is the culmination of years of disobedience rebellion and idolatry. Israel and Judah now find themselves in captivity in Assyria and Babylon. Israel's loss of victory came because the presence of God was conditional on the fulfillment of the temple sacrifices and their obedience to the laws of Moses. Under David they achieved the very best possible within the Mosaic covenant but even David fell into adultery and murder bringing upon the nation warfare and instability. Psalm 46:5 states that since "God is within her (Jerusalem) she will not fall." Yet we have a vivid description of Nebuchadnezzar's conquest and destruction of Jerusalem in second Kings 25. We understand from this Old Covenant lesson that God's presence was conditional on the obedience of men and therefore it was not sustainable but for the shortest periods of time.

It is this question of sustainable victory that troubles so many who have entered the New Covenant in and through the Lord Jesus Christ. It is not at all difficult to compare one's experience in Christ with that of the Israelites under the Old Covenant. Many Christians identify with Paul's words in Romans seven:

> For I have the desire to do what is good but I cannot carry it out. For what I do is not the good I want to do; no, the evil I do not want to do – this I keep on doing.

(Romans 7:18-20)

Paul goes on to describe the war that goes on inside every Christian:

> So I find this law at work: When I want to do good, evil is right there with me. For in my inner being I delight in God's law but I see another law at work in the members of my body, waging war against the law of my mind and making me a prisoner of the law of sin at work in my members. What a wretched man I am! Who will rescue me from this body of death? (Romans 7:21-24)

When Paul speaks of "my inner being" he is referring to that inner temple where the Holy Spirit has taken up residence with the express purpose of growing and maturing our new inner man into the fullness of the image of Christ. Indeed, it is ever helpful to see the new birth as a moment of conception and our inner temple as a womb in which the new man is undergoing a gestation that will culminate in "the creations'" completed "expectation for the sons of God to be revealed." (Romans 8:19) But he also declares there is "another law" making me a prisoner of the law of sin." (vs. 23)

This is where there is a two-fold confusion encountered by Christians who have not yet lived out the victory that is ours in Christ. Remember that Psalm 46 tells us that the city will not fall because of the presence of God. If, as Paul says we are a temple of God and that the Spirit of God lives in us, why then do we still find ourselves "prisoners" to the law of sin. Every Christian knows what Paul is saying in Romans seven to be true from personal experience. We fall daily if not hourly to this truth.

23

We assume then that the Spirit has left us because of our sin and then climb into a religious hamster wheel whose purpose is for us to regain God's favor and presence. If we have been saved from sin through Christ's death on the cross why then does sin still seem to have the upper hand in our lives? Christians tend to shape their theology and doctrine to conform to their experience. This is an area where false teaching and false understanding prevails. Faced with Romans 7 it is easy to accept defeat now with the promise of victory someday in heaven, leaving us weak and discouraged with little Kingdom impact in this world. Where then is this victory promised to those who live in the presence of God?

Jesus made the answer abundantly clear when he said, "I am the way, the truth and the life." No greater truth was ever spoken and yet so rarely fully understood. Victory is in Christ. It never was nor could it ever be in us. Some look for power conferred upon them that they might use it to achieve victory. Others seek knowledge as a tool or a formula for victory. Deep within our culture is the belief that given enough resources, energy and know-how we can solve any problem or defeat any enemy. Ours is a "how-to" and a "self-help" world that is at cross-purposes with the kingdom of God. In the Kingdom it is no longer how but Who, neither is it self but Him and Him alone.

Another misunderstanding in our view of Him and His work is that He died to give us a fresh new start. The slate has been wiped clean and now, with his assistance through Holy Spirit power and gifts we can meet the challenge of God-pleasing holiness in a fallen world. This fails to grasp the fundamental reality of our brokenness and complete incompetence and our continuing dependence on Christ after the initiating work of regeneration has taken place. Paul expressed the meaning of this in Philippians. "And I am sure of this, that He who has begun a good work in you, will bring it to completion until the day of Jesus Christ." (1:6)

The Lord does not just give us a hand up. He promises to go the distance with us and continue the work He has started. Why? The Lord lovingly saves us because we are utterly helpless to save ourselves. This condition of helplessness continues after the new birth. This is what Paul is describing in Romans Seven. The new birth does not turn us into unconquerable warriors for the Kingdom of God. It begins a process in which our lives are surrendered completely to the One who alone is the victor over sin and death. Only He defeated sin and death and only He can win victory in and through our surrendered lives. Christ does not equip us. He dwells within and does His work as we surrender our will to His.

Some have called this the exchanged life. I give my life to Him and He gives His to me. Jesus spoke of this in Luke 6:38-39.

> And whoever does not take up his cross and follow me is not worthy of me. Whoever finds his life will lose it and whoever loses his life for my sake will find it.

This is the exchange. Christ has called us to die to self, to lose our life for His sake. This means I give up my dreams, hopes and expectations and in exchange I receive His. The confusion over this exchange is in the misunderstanding of death to self. It has been portrayed in many false guises and teachings as a means of gaining merit or favour with God. Evangelicals who stand on the finished work of Christ are naturally repelled by this notion, though even we manage to create our own religious works in order to please God. At first the exchange appears to be a sacrifice unless we understand that we are giving over our old broken and incompetent life in exchange for His victorious one. Christ offers Himself to us. Many settle for keeping their old lives and engage in the pursuit of spiritual experiences and gifts they hope will enable them to win a battle that was long ago lost. A new paint job and new tires won't fix a broken axle and a blown engine. We need a new vehicle, "Therefore, if anyone is in Christ, he is a new creation; the old has gone, the new has come! (2 Corinthians 5:17) and a new driver. Jesus answered, "I am the way and the truth and the life. No one comes to the Father except through me." (John 14:6)

The exchanged life is not about Jesus as a model or example but the indwelling Christ living his life in me and through me. Death to self quite naturally repels and frightens us but it becomes increasingly attractive as we endure the endless parade of failure and efforts to win victory in our own strength.

It is unfortunate that so few discover the joy of finding Jesus' words in Matthew 11:28-30 to be wonderfully true.

> "Come to me all you who are weary and burdened, and I will give you rest. Take my yoke upon you and learn from me, for I am gentle and humble in heart, and you will find rest for your souls. For my yoke is easy and my burden is light."

The writer to the Hebrews expressed the meaning of this when he said: "…for anyone who enters God's rest, also rests from his own work…" (4:10). Christ offers to do all of the work in and through us and in so doing we find rest for our souls. He cannot fail. We always fail and always will as long as we try to do the work of the kingdom ourselves.

This is why Paul's answer to Romans 7:24-25 is simple and clear. "Who will rescue me from this body of death? Thanks be to God – through Jesus Christ our Lord." (24-25). These words transition the reader to the glorious victories in Romans 8. Romans 8 is what the victorious life looks like:

1. Christ Jesus sets us free from the law of sin and death. Meaning no condemnation to those in Christ Jesus. What we were and are powerless to do God did and does still. (8: 1-4)
2. By the Holy Spirit the misdeeds of the body are put to death. Don't miss the idea of death: something that is dead is finished. Victory over Romans seven is ours in Christ. (8:12-17)
3. The Holy Spirit in us prays for us according to the will of God. (8:26-27)
4. The sovereign God has predestined us to become like Christ. He calls, He justifies, He glorifies. (8:28-30)
5. Because of all this none can be against us and all things are ours in Christ. We live in triumphant victory no matter what happens to us because nothing can separate us from the love of God. (8:31-39)

There are many possible reasons for being a Christian and living in defeat. There are two that bring the truth of the victorious life into focus.

1. You don't know what Christ has done for you and thus you have settled for less than "all the riches in the Heavenly place in Christ."
2. Because you have not come to understand that victory, (past, present and future) resides only in Christ you have continued after the new birth to work for victory in your own strength.

Many of us have unknowingly opened ourselves to the charge against the "foolish

Galatians."

> "Are you so foolish? After beginning with the spirit, are you now trying to attain your goal by human effort?"
> Galatians 3:3

We know well Ephesians 2:8-9, "For by grace you have been saved through faith and that not of yourselves, it is the gift of God, not of works…" Whether the return is to Judaism and the law, as the Galatians did, matters not if we live by "human effort." Christ died because we were and are utterly incapable of saving ourselves. The new birth does not confer upon us a new competence. It incorporates us into the body of the One who alone is victorious.

Salvation is "a gift of God" and so is the victorious life. When you prayed on the day of your conversion you asked for the gift of salvation. There was no other remedy and no one else to go to but Christ, the way, the truth, the life. It is the same principle that must guide us in living the rest of our life in Christ. We come to Him and ask in utter submission and dependence for His continuous work of grace, an exchange of our will for His, our life for His, our weakness for His strength, our defeat for His victory.

If you have lived in defeat for all of your Christian life and know it to be so, it is possible that you are coming to the place where you are ready to exchange your life for His. A gift must be asked for and received. This gift is given to those who know they need it and are willing to ask for it. "Ask and you shall receive, seek and you will find, knock and the door will be opened." Matthew 7:7.

Chapter Three
The Pursuit of God

In his classic book "The Sacrament of the Present Moment" Jean-Pierre De Caussade said that Christians spend their lives looking everywhere for spiritual food but God. Psalm 105:4 says "Look to the Lord and His strength; seek His face always." We are struck as we read the Psalms by the psalmists' passion to pursue God.

> One thing I ask of the Lord, this is what I seek: That I may dwell in the house of the Lord all the days of my life, to gaze upon the beauty of the Lord and to seek Him is His temple. (Psalm 27:4)

Paul echoes this single-mindedness in Philippians 3.

> ...One thing I do: Forgetting what is behind and straining toward what is ahead, I press on toward the goal to win the prize for which God has called me heavenward in Christ Jesus. (3:14)

Our God has passionately and relentlessly pursued us to redeem and love us and now we find ourselves running after Him like the Shulamite in Song of Solomon. It appears that at the moment of the new birth, the divine seed of life, having been sown in our being, restlessly and persistently seeks out its source. Because God is love and He has created us anew in His image it is in our very spiritual DNA to return the love He has given. Indeed, it should be the consuming passion of every child of God. The Lord illustrated the expected response in the parables of the hidden treasure and the pearl in Matthew.

> The kingdom of Heaven is like treasure hidden in a field. When a man found it, he hid it again, and then in his joy went and sold all he had and bought that field. Again, the Kingdom of Heaven is like a merchant looking for fine pearls. When he found one of great value, he went away and sold everything he had and bought it. (Matthew 13:44-46)

It was Christ's expectation that those who find the true treasure, the joy of intimacy and love in the Father, would give everything they have in exchange for it, that they would drop their own dreams, aspirations, plans, in exchange for pursuing God as their life's one passion. Nothing would be too much to give "to grasp how wide and long and high and deep is the love of Christ, and to know this love that surpasses knowledge – that, you may be filled to the measure of all the fullness of God." (Ephesians 3:18, 19)

And yet there are still many who love this world more than the One who died for them and there are those who find themselves mired in the defeat described in Romans seven, powerless to let go of the things in the flesh and yet longing for more of the life of Christ.

Andrew Murray expressed this divided life experience in his book The Prayer Life.

> "There are many who place their hope for salvation in the redemption of the cross who understand little about the

> fellowship of the cross. They rely on what the cross has purchased for them, on forgiveness of sin and peace with God; but they can often live for a length of time without fellowship with the Lord himself. They do not know what it means to strive every day after having communion with the crucified Lord as He is seen in Heaven – "A lamb in the midst of the throne." Oh that this vision might exercise its spiritual power upon us, that we might experience every day…the power and experience of His presence here." [2]

Forgiveness of sin, the new birth are not an end but a beginning. The legal question of our sin is settled by the sacrifice of Christ but many miss the true purpose behind Christ's work. God is love. This is not a description of an attribute of God but the very definition of His being. He created man in Genesis to share His love both in giving and receiving. Adam's fall broke the relationship. From that moment God's express purpose was to bring us back into that communion of love. At the moment of the new birth the relationship is re-established and we can freely choose to receive from and give love to our Father in heaven. To know Him is to love Him. Salvation should be the moment we fall in love with God and a lifelong pursuit of Him should begin.

Those who have fallen in love with their future spouses have some sense of what this means. Remember how you wanted to spend every free moment with your beloved, who became the sole focus of your time and energy. Your passion became a pursuit with the consummation of your relationship as your ultimate goal. This is

---

[2] Andrew Murray, <u>The Prayer Life</u> (Chicago: Moody Press), 116.

what it means to pursue God, a desire to continually be with Him and to get to know Him and ultimately to live in full union with Him. The scholars and doctors of the church have explained well all the doctrines of the salvation experience. We know of atonement, redemption, and grace. We know about the charismatic gifts, regeneration, sanctification and eschatology. If our relationship with God were based on our understanding of doctrine and theology we would all pass the exam. But it is not and was never meant to be. You would never be satisfied in a relationship with only an accurate description of your beloved. You want, you desire the real person. This is our true gift in Christ. He prayed in John 17 to the Father "…That they may be one as we are one." (Vs. 11) This is not just a legal standing but also an actual one for those in Christ. Someone once described Christians as adopted children waiting in the orphanage. The papers have all been signed and we are just waiting for father to pick us up. This implies that the relational part of our new standing is in the future, a very wrong description of what it means to be in Christ. By 'one' He meant that we would walk in the same relationship with the Father as He did when He was among us, with all the implied intimacy and interaction that sustained His mission and His Sonship. We are God's children <u>now</u>. Eternal life has already begun and so has access to our Father in Heaven. "<u>All</u> the riches in the Heavenly places are (ours)…in Christ." When Paul spoke of the Holy Spirit as "first fruits" (Romans 8) and "the guarantee of our inheritance until we acquire possession of it," he did not intend us to understand him as saying we get a "sample taste" designed to get us thinking of "the 'fullness' of the Spirit and all the fullness of Christ." In other words there is available to us now all we can possibly handle in this world. It was He who said "Eye has not seen nor ear heard, neither has entered into the heart of man the things which God has prepared for those who love Him." This means that the future of our love relationship with God is beyond our comprehension. The good news, however, is that it starts now.

It is the question of pursuing or seeking that is unclear to so many. An unfortunate distortion of the truth lies in the notion that God is distant and only approachable to a few elite spiritual giants, those in missions, or monasteries or the specially called. Such persons are seen to have the luxury of hours of prayer and bible study unchallenged by the humdrum realities of living in the "real" world like the rest of us. They can give themselves fully to the ministry of the word and prayer while we concern ourselves with the practical necessities of keeping body and soul together. God bless them! We'll support them. We might even pray for them from time to time. This belief absolves us from the responsibility to pursue God ourselves, which may account for its general acceptance in Christian practice. One who follows the pursuit of the beloved in Song of Songs can see that it is by analogy an endeavor beset with both joys and frustrations, and that it is continuous.

The pursuit of our beloved God is like trying to catch a deer on the mountain slopes, dangerous, exhilarating and characterized by many perceived failures along with surprising, unanticipated successes. It is the starting point that eludes so many. Where does one begin to seek God? The answer is closer than one might ever imagine. He is found in His temple, always in His temple. "Know you not that you are the temple of God and that His Spirit dwells in you?" He is as close as your beating heart and waiting for you to enter into His temple and commune with Him and He with you.

One of our best teachers in this practice is Moses. In Exodus 33 we learn that he went daily, sometimes for long periods to meet with the Lord in "The Tent of Meeting." The Lord promised to dwell in the midst of the Israelites during their journey to the Promised Land.

> "My presence will go with you and I will give you rest."
> Exodus 33:14

His chosen dwelling and meeting place was "The Tent of Meeting" and ultimately the tabernacle, "A copy and shadow of what is in Heaven." (Exodus 8:5) Now we are that true tabernacle, the tent of meeting, and the dwelling place of the Living God. Just like Moses it is our privilege to go to that place and meet with God as long as or as much as we want.

> "Now Moses used to take a tent and pitch it outside the camp some distance away, calling it the 'Tent of Meeting.'" Exodus 33:7
>
> "As Moses went into the tent, the pillar of cloud would come down and stay at the entrance, while the Lord spoke with Moses. The Lord would speak to Moses face to face, as a man speaks with his friend." Exodus 33:9, 11

This is the pillar of cloud that went with all Israel as they traveled which came down to this meeting place for a personal encounter with Moses. They spoke face to face as friends would speak to one another. There are two ways to look at this. The first is that Moses was a spiritual giant and attained this special status because of his godliness and dedication. Of course, we need to remember that he fled Egypt as a murderer and was called by God out of a 40-year sojourn shepherding sheep. It's hard to find any special qualifications Moses had that would bring him to this privileged place of friendship with God. The second approach is to remember the words of the writer to the Hebrews as he reflected on this very ministry Moses carried out.

> "Jesus has become the guarantee of the better covenant."
> Hebrews 7:22

In fact "better" is the operative word all though Hebrews as the writer compares what we have in Christ with the covenant under Moses – better revelation (1:4), better end (6:0), better hope (7:15), better priesthood (7:7), better mediator (8:6), better promises (8:6), better sacrifice (9:23), better forever (10:34). The point is that, as good as it was with Moses it is far better with us in Christ. As the Lord's temple we do not have to go to a specifically designated place and wait for a cloud. We already have the indwelling presence of that very same One who met with Moses. In fact our relationship with the Father is based on Christ's standing, not just as our "better" mediator, but also as the Son of God. Moses was a servant in the house of the Lord but Christ was faithful as a Son over God's house. (Hebrews 3:6) We come to the Father as His children, no longer as slaves or servants.

There is one critical observation in the life of Moses observed again in the life of the Lord that answers the question raised by this understanding of this opportunity to commune with God. Why is it that so few Christians know the reality of meeting with God in personal intimacy? One scripture cited in the life of Moses is central to understanding his knowledge of God.

> Now Moses was a very humble man, more humble than
> anyone on the face of the earth. (Numbers 12:3)

One who knew of this intimacy with God wrote that the doorway to friendship with God is humility. Miguel De Molinos wrote that the way of sanctification is humiliation. This is rooted in the original breach between God and a created being –

Satan.

> "So often it is through sheer weakness that man does not open himself to grace; but Satan shut himself off from love by an absolutely deliberate refusal sprung from his pride. He was stopped short by the first, the most essential of love's demands: He would not enter into the mystery of charity because it is the mystery of humility." [3]

God's love is offered to us freely but we cannot accept it without being changed by it. The essence of pride is the desire to remain independent and self-sufficient, to owe one's happiness to our own power to achieve it. God's love cannot be negotiated on our own terms. It must be received unconditionally on his terms. It is this fear of losing ourselves our personal autonomy, which keeps us from entering the temple of the Lord to meet with Him. Adam and Eve illustrate this principle well. They hid from the Lord because they knew that coming into His presence would mean exposure and accountability for their actions. This residual fear and shame remains even in Christians. Sometimes it is justified by a lifestyle lacking in obedience and holiness but still for most, if not all of us, the old self-life fights to retain control even after it's real death on the cross.

> "I have been crucified with Christ and I no longer live, but Christ lives in me. The life I live in the body, I live by faith in the Son of God, who loved me and gave himself for me." (Galatians 2:20)

---

[3] Georges Lefebvre, <u>The Mystery of God's Love</u> (Great Britain: Sheed & Ward, 1961), 15.

So it is either fear of the exposure or loss of autonomy that deters Christians from entering the inner chamber of their temple. Of course those fears are unreasonable in view of who God is. He has shown His love by laying down His life for us. The perceived loss of self is actually quite real but what is offered is an exchange – our old broken corrupted self for the life of Christ. In His love God gives us infinitely more than He asks us to give up. The old self does not go easily but it can be done if we are willing to surrender to His loving work in our hearts.

Christ followed this path before us and thus has called us to take up our cross and follow Him in the path of surrender to the Father's will. He lovingly promises to teach and mentor us in the way in Matthew 11:28-30.

> "Come to me, all you who are weary and burdened, and I will give you rest. Take my yoke upon on you and learn from me, for I am gentle and humble in heart, and you will find rest for your souls. For my yoke is easy and my burden is light." Matthew 11:28-30.

As our humble teacher He is calling us to the same path of humility that He walked. This is the way to the inner chamber – not my will but yours Father, not my way but yours Lord.

Chapter Four
The Will of God

In my earliest days of ministry we would hold conferences and put on workshops on the various aspects of Christian discipleship. Invariably the one workshop that was over-subscribed was entitled "How to Know the Will of God." This remains as one of the great questions every believer would like a simple answer to, especially since this subject is further clouded by a persistent inability to do the will of God. Failure to know and to do naturally breeds confusion. Jesus declared that we would know the truth and that the truth would set us free. (John 8:32) Is this a failed promise or a failure of apprehension?

Actually one of the causes of misunderstanding God's will is rooted in our practice of prayer. Most of us are conversant with prayer promises like "Ask and you shall receive that your joy may be full." (John 16:24) Rarely is this promise combined with:

> "If you remain in me and my words remain in you, ask whatever you wish and it will be given to you? John 15:7

Or

> "Do not conform any longer to the pattern of this world, but be transformed by the renewing of your mind. Then you will be able to test and approve what God's will is – His good, pleasing and perfect will. Romans 12:2

We are eager to take the promises of answered prayer and run with them and at the same time reluctant to engage in an intimate relationship with God that we might have and know His will. So many pray using verses like John 16:24, "Until now, you have not asked for anything in my name. Ask and you will receive, and your joy will be complete," only to find that there is a lot of asking and very little receiving, hence the question "What then is God's will?" A common experience is one of praying for someone's salvation based on 2 Peter 3:9.

> "(God is)… not willing that any should perish but that all should come to repentance."

It is reasonable to conclude that since God wants everyone to be saved it must be His will for us to pray for the lost and there is a guarantee that our prayer will be answered. After all, it is His will. But our experience does not bear this out. Not everyone we pray for gets saved. Indeed it seems that very few and sometimes none are saved. There must be a flaw in our logic somewhere. John 15:7 is a starting point for answering our question. What is God's will? What does it mean then to remain in or "abide" in Christ's word(s)?

John is near the climax of Jesus' farewell discourse to his disciples. He has already made clear to them what it means to abide in Christ - keeping His commandments.

> If you love me you will obey what I command. John 14:15
> Whoever has my commands and obeys them he is the one who loves me. John 14:21
> If anyone loves me he will obey my teachings. John 14:23
> If you obey my commands you will remain in my love. John 15:10
> You are my friends if you do what I command. John

15:14

If you abide you will have what you ask establishes out of the very mouth of our Lord an unassailable link between obedience and answered prayer. We live in a time of easy believism based on a distorted perception of grace. Salvation, not by works (Ephesians 2:8-9) has been wrongfully projected into a grace-based Christian life without works.

James spoke of this false understanding of the Christian life in his epistle.

> Do not merely listen to the word, and so deceive yourselves. Do what it says. James 1:22

I have already cited Romans 12:1-2 which links this life of obedience to knowing the will of God. John gives his own version in his first epistle.

> Do not love the world or anything in the world. If anyone loves the world, the love of the Father is not in him. For everything in the world – the cravings of sinful man, the lust of his eyes and the boasting of what he has done and does – comes not from the Father but from the world. 2 John 2:15-16

One of the reasons, particularly for evangelicals, that we have gone into an extreme position on grace is our fear of becoming religious – of legalism. This is rooted in the false belief that the will of God will unfold as another series of rules and laws for us to keep. Jesus' teachings were never intended to take us back into law but forward into a dynamic relationship with God. Man's relationship with God broke down when law was written in stone rather than on his heart. Jeremiah, speaking of the new covenant, prophesied that our new relationship with God would be a heart relationship.

> "This is the covenant I will make with the house of Israel after that time," declares the Lord. "I will put my law in their minds and write it on their hearts. I will be their God, and they will be my people." Jeremiah 31:33

The old covenant was mediated by scripture and obedience to the law. The new is mediated by the relationship of the Son to the Father. We come to the Father in Him with a heart transformed by the regenerating work of Holy Spirit and now we find ourselves in a living dynamic relationship with God. His will is no longer written in stone but is revealed continuously in the context of knowing and interacting with Him. The legalist would rather have a set of rules like those in Mitzvot, the 613 Jewish commandments intended to cover every possible ethical, legal and spiritual situation a Jew might encounter. Thus he would always know the right thing to do – the will of God for all of life's possibilities. Paul succinctly declared the flaw in this approach. "The sting of death is sin, and the power of sin is the law." (2 Corinthians 15:56) Law actually empowers our sinful nature and inevitably produces death.

How then can we know the will of God in a life giving, freeing way. Jesus declares Himself alone to be the way, the truth, and the life. His purpose was to bring us face to face with the Father as sons and daughters who learn from Him moment by moment through relationship His living will. There must be a conversation for this to take place and thus we come to the meaning and purpose of prayer – conversation with the Father. It is in the conversations that we discover His will. Prayer is how we discover the will of God.

Simone Weill in her discourse on the Lord's Prayer linked 'thy will be done' with 'give us this day our daily bread'. Thy will be done is our commitment to the will of God past, present and future. It is a declaration of submission, of saying as our Lord did, not my will but Yours (the Father's) be done. In asking for our daily bread she called it a request for "God's will nourished by the Holy Spirit." Thus to fully know the will of God we must begin by surrendering our own will and seeking only the Father's. This is, in fact, the core of the Lord's Prayer, the very emphasis He wanted His disciples to grasp if they were to be effective in their prayer lives. The fundamental posture of abiding is a life conformed to the will of God. And as John 15:7 states it is a requisite for answered prayer.

> "If you remain in me and my words remain in you, ask whatever you wish, and it will be given you." John 15:7

There is great difficulty in fully surrendering to the Father's will. Even the Lord Jesus wrestled with final and full surrender to the Father in Gethsemane. This is the lesson of Job who spent days complaining about what God had done to him unfairly. Then the Father speaks:

> "Who is this that darkens my counsel with words without knowledge." Job 38:1
> "Will the one who contends with the almighty correct him? Let him who accuses God answer Him." Job 40:1

Job began with a classic legalistic approach to God. He excelled in prayer, sacrifice and a righteous lifestyle but it unfolds as we read the whole story that Job was simply doing those things that would bring God's favor and blessing. His heart was right but he lacked an intimate and personal relationship with God. In religious practice he excelled above all his contemporaries but he did not know God, hence his climactic revelation.

> "My ears had heard of you but now my eyes have seen you." Job 42:5

This was the real purpose of all that Job had gone through, to move him from the law to the heart, from religion to relationship. This is God's purpose for every one of His children.

The backdrop to this was Job's discovery of the absolute sovereignty of God. Even Satan was under the Father's domination and control. In chapters 38 through 42 God essentially declares that everything is His will and under His control from the hatching of an egg to the leviathan in the sea, the sun and moon and stars, the seasons and all that mankind does.

> "He looks down on the haughty; He is King over all that are proud." (Job 41:34)

Our attachment to our own will reflects a failure to apprehend the truth that everything is God's will. Jesus echoed this in the Sermon on the Mount saying such things as "He sees the sparrow fall to the ground." The very hairs on your head are numbered." He has a name for every star in the sky. Surrender to the will of God is simply the act of recognizing the inevitable, of aligning one's life with reality. But one must lay down all of his own will to receive the fullness of the Father's will. The Psalmist speaks of this truth.

> "The Lord's will stands fast forever and the designs of his heart from age to age. " Psalm 33:11

He who chooses to retain His own will enters into a battle he cannot win. We are free to do God's will but we are not free to interfere with it. This tends to raise the age-old question of free will versus the sovereignty of God. There isn't a simple answer. Indeed these two truths, which are both found in scripture, must remain in a dynamic tension. The real issue is where the best and safest place for us to be exists. Why "contend with the Almighty" as Job did when the possibility of abiding under the shadow of the Almighty is open to all who choose His will.

Jesus' remarkable calm in a storm that frightened experienced Sea of Galilee fishermen illustrates that living in the center of God's will is the safest place in the universe. Knowing that He was perfectly in the Father's will gave Him the peace to sleep through a life-threatening storm. He said in John 6:38:

> "For I have come down from Heaven not to do my will but to do the will of Him who sent me."

He lived his whole life in the exact center of the Father's will. That is the place we would all love to be but it is one that ranges from difficult to impossible to find. We must remember to focus on the whole of Jesus' incarnational ministry if we wish to discover the answer to this apparent mystery. We know His words in Gethsemane, "Not my will but yours" but forget that the surrender of His will began at the moment He accepted the Father's plan for Him to take on our humanity.

> Your attitude should be the same as that of Jesus Christ: Who, being in very nature God did not consider equality with God something to be grasped, but made himself nothing, taking the very nature of a servant, being made in human likeness. And being found in appearance as a man, he humbled himself and became obedient to death – even death on a cross! Philippians 2:5-8

Since Jesus walked the path of complete obedience in taking on our humanity He succeeded in our behalf where we could not. His call to abide in Him is the call to dwell in the one and only place we can actually live out the Father's will. – In Him. He is the vine. We are the branches. It is the flow of his life in and through us that brings the victory that is impossible apart from Him. "Apart from me you can do nothing." (John 15:5)

How do we abide? We must make the same decision, the same commitment that He did. We must exchange our will for that of the Father and, as Philippians two demands, embrace an attitude the same as that of Jesus. We must make ourselves nothing in order for the Father's will to become everything to us.

The bad news is that we are not even capable of doing this; such is our weakness and depraved nature. The good news is God has given us prayer so that we can ask Him to work in us to will to do His good pleasure. The Psalmist expressed this utter dependence on the Father's work in his heart,

> "Teach me your way, O Lord, that I may walk in your truth; give me an undivided heart that I may fear your name." Psalm 86:11

The Psalmist acknowledged that His heart was divided. Paul repeated this in his writings. Romans 7 describes this division. The good that I want to do I do not do. The evil I would not that I do. Paul is actually saying that we have within us two wills. Our heart is divided between the will of God, which exists in the new creation in Christ, and the will of the old self, which though crucified with Christ (Galatians 2:20) remains in opposition to God. Paul's answer to this war is Christ. Thanks be to God who through Christ sets us free from this warfare and transforms our heart by removing the division. Thus the Psalmist could speak of a transformation.

> "I delight to do your will, O my God, your law is within my heart." Psalm 40:8

Thus prayer is not about finding the will of God but about asking God to conform us to His will – "give me an undivided heart that I may fear your name". It is in being transformed and thus abiding in Christ that we begin to experience and live out the Father's will. Prayer is about the surrender of our will to God so that it can be replaced by His. There is no other way to know the will of God.

Jacob was a man who never actually surrendered to the will of God. He wrestled with God all the days of his life for the blessing that was already his. Perhaps he learned this from his mother Rebecca who was told by God in a dream that Isaac's blessing would go to the younger of the twins. Yet she was unwilling to let God work out His promise and she took matters into her own hands. Jacob never got free of this. Even with God's blessing He never stopped manipulating in order to gain, by his own efforts, God's promise. The scene in Genesis 32:22-33 where he wrestles with God illustrates how he had lived his life. Instead of worshipping and inquiring of God he took hold of Him and wrestled for a blessing that had already been conferred in his dream at Bethel in Genesis 28:13-15 twenty years before this encounter. His refusal to trust in and rest in the will of God resulted in misery in his marriages, betrayal by his own children and years of sorrow and suffering, hence his confession before Pharaoh.

> And Jacob said to Pharaoh, "The years of my pilgrimage are a hundred and thirty. My years have been few and difficult, and they do not equal the years of the pilgrimage of my fathers." Genesis 47:9

Though he spent his lifetime living physically in the will of God he never experienced the rest and peace in his heart that would come if he surrendered in faith and trust as Abraham before him had.

> "Yet he did not waver through unbelief regarding the promise of God but was strengthened in his faith and gave glory to God." Romans 4:20

Christ is willing and able to keep us fully in the Father's will safely under the shadow of His mighty wings. In prayer we offer Him our submission and our trust. We have been given by our Father "all the blessings in the Heavenly places." (Ephesians

1:3) He will finish what He has started. (Philippians 1:6). Of this we can be certain. Let us not be like Jacob who ended up exactly where God had promised Abraham 215 years before. Yet he never surrendered his heart and thus his trust to God's will. Let us say to Him who gave His all for us. "Not my will but Yours".

Chapter Five

The Cross of Christ

Luke 23 recounts the story of the two criminals crucified with Christ. In a way this story gives us a perspective that might be called the two sides of the cross. The one criminal who reviled Jesus was goading Him into proving His divinity by saving both Himself and the reviler.

> "Aren't you the Christ? Save yourself and us!" But the other criminal rebuked him. "Don't you fear God, " he said, "Since you are under the same sentence? We are punished justly, for we are getting what our deeds deserve. But this man has done nothing wrong." Then he said, "Jesus, remember me when you come into your kingdom." Jesus answered him, "I tell you the truth, today you will be with me in paradise." Luke 23:34-43

The first criminal saw Jesus as someone who might be used to escape punishment and suffering that he believed was unfair and undeserved. The other saw Jesus as merciful and loving and knew he was getting what he deserved. The first thief's perspective, the utilitarian view of Jesus, prevails in our churches today. The cross is not something to be embraced but avoided and Christ's role is to either prevent or ease suffering.

Simone Weill said, "The extreme greatness of Christianity is that it does not seek a supernatural cure for suffering, but a supernatural use of it."[4] It is the role of suffering, particularly a sound theology of the cross that eludes modern evangelical minds. We prefer a theology of glory, Christ's purpose being to promote our happiness, well-being, and success. These are the new measures of God's blessing on our lives. Those who suffer must be under judgment or divine punishment for some failure or lack of faith in the goodness of God.

We all want glory but there is no shortcut around the way of the cross. One must learn the way of the cross before the way of exaltation and glory. Why? Because this is the way that our Savior walked and He has invited us to follow Him in it.

> Then Jesus said to his disciples, "If anyone would come after me, he must deny himself and take up his cross and follow me." Matthew 16:24

This is a sweeping invitation that includes all those who call themselves Christians. There does not appear to be room for any other kind of Christ follower but for those who deny self and take up their cross.

Paul clarified the meaning of this in Philippians two by exhorting us to be of the same mind as Christ who denied himself, became a servant of the Father's will and laid down his life.

> "Therefore God has highly exalted Him and bestowed on Him the name that is above every name," (Philippians 2:9)

---

[4] Simone Weill, Gravity and Grace (Routledge: New York, 1999), xxviii.

Christ walked the path of the cross and this led to glory. His call for us to take up our cross means that the pattern our life is to follow that of His.

> The Spirit Himself bears witness with our spirit that we are children of God, and if children, then heirs – heirs of God and fellow heirs with Christ, <u>provided we suffer with Him in order that we may also be glorified with Him</u>.
> Romans 8:16-17

The call to take up the cross is not just a thread in Scripture, it is a highway through Christ's teaching and all the Spirit inspired writers of the epistles.

The failure to teach this fundamental truth of discipleship lies in its unattractive appeal. It is the quickest way to clear a church or bring disfavor on one's pulpit ministry. Few want to hear about self-denial and death to self. At the same time there is little reluctance to have a ministry like Paul with all the attendant signs and wonders, souls saved and churches planted. However he himself declared his desire to…

> … know Him and the power of His resurrection and … share His sufferings becoming like Him in His death.
> (Philippians 3:10)

Paul knew that his ministry was based on his surrender to Christ's call to take up his cross. His life is a testimony to this reality if one is to believe his description of his many tests and sufferings in 2 Corinthians 11.

> Are they servants of Christ? I am a better one – I am talking like a madman – with far greater labors, far more imprisonments, with countless beatings, and often near death. Five times I received at the hand of the Jews the forty lashes less one. Three times I was beaten with rods. Once I was stoned. Three times I was shipwrecked; a night and a day I was adrift at sea; on frequent journeys, in danger from rivers, danger from robbers…2 Corinthians 11:23-29

These experiences did not put God in his debt. They were very simply the result of following Christ. He obeyed the Father and these experiences were the result, as of course was all the fruit of his lengthy ministry. One of the clearest illustrations of this is found in Acts 16.

> Paul and his companions traveled throughout the region of Phrygia and Galatia having been kept by the Holy Spirit from preaching the word in the province of Asia. When they came to the border of Mysia they tried to enter Bithynia, but the Spirit of Jesus would not allow them to. So they passed by Mysia and went down to Troas. During the night Paul had a vision of a man of Macedonia standing and begging him, "Come over to Macedonia and help us." After Paul had seen the vision, we got ready at once to leave for Macedonia, concluding that God had called us to preach the gospel to them."

This is a marvelous story of the leading of the Holy Spirit excepting that it led Paul to Philippi where he and Silas were beaten and imprisoned in chains for the very preaching of the gospel God had called them to in Philippi. Now the result was the conversion of the Philippian jailer and his entire household but the only way we can make sense of this is that God directed Paul specifically into this situation with the express intention of saving the jailer knowing that it would cost his messengers a beating and a night in chains. Paul, in the most concrete way, truly experienced the fulfillment of his desire to become like Christ in His death.

Was this a special call on the life of perhaps the greatest of the church's apostles, a one and only, never to be repeated story of discipleship? Not at all. Paul taught the Corinthians and undoubtedly all of his other children to follow the same pattern of the cross.

> Follow my example, as I follow the example of Christ. 1 Corinthians 11:1

This is based on a simple principle for every follower of Christ. We must partake of His death if we wish to partake of His life. Paul speaks of this in his epistle to the Galatians.

> I have been crucified with Christ and I no longer live but Christ lives in me. The life I live in the body I live by faith in the Son of God who loved me and gave himself for me. Galatians 2:20.

Paul speaks of an absolute truth not an expression of legalism in the form of doctrine. Every born again believer is and was in fact crucified with Christ. This is the meaning of our very real position "in Christ." It is easier to think of this teaching in doctrinal or legal terms than to appropriate the truth that we are actually in Christ. God has spiritually incorporated us into the body of Christ giving us a share in the cross in order that we may participate in the resurrection.

> Or don't you know that all of us who were baptized into Christ Jesus were baptized into His death? We were therefore buried with Him through baptism into death in order that, just as Christ was raised from the dead through the glory of the Father, we too may live a new life. Romans 6:3-5.

If then we have died with Him, why then does He call His disciples to take up their cross and follow Him? He is calling us to conform our lives to the work of the cross, to the actual truth that has made us new creations in Christ – to live the crucified life.

The crucified life is patterned by the Lord himself, a life of self-denial given over completely to the will of the Father. Two difficulties attend. The first is that it is entirely impossible for us to live the crucified life. A Kempis' title to his classic book, <u>The Imitation of Christ,</u> can mislead. We cannot imitate Christ. Many have tried and all have failed. The Galatians succumbed to this temptation to return to working out salvation in the flesh even though they had begun in the Spirit. Many have followed them into this snare and experienced the heartbreak and frustration of repeated failure. It is our very inability to save ourselves that aroused the love of God to send His Son to die for us. And yet He still had to give Himself willingly to the cross. Even Christ could not crucify Himself. He alone could and did do in that second garden what Adam failed to do. He surrendered His will and obeyed. It is this that we are incapable of even as God's children. By this I mean we cannot give ourselves over to the cross of our own will. We must ask God to supernaturally do what we cannot. The cross itself illustrates. One could nail his own feet to the cross and even one hand but that last nail is a physical impossibility and thus must be the work of another.

It is in the second difficulty that we discover the key. Paul says in Romans 6:

> "In the same way count yourselves dead to sin but alive to
> God in Christ." Romans 6:5.

The KJV says "reckon yourselves" meaning consider yourself dead. Live your life as one crucified with Christ. The key to this is our will and the consequent transformation of our mind so that we live out our lives in concord with the will of God. This is the crucified life.

> "For it is God who works in you to will and act according
> to His purpose." Philippians 2:13

If I was crucified with Christ and He commands me to take up my cross and live the crucified life, to consider myself dead, then I must first accept my identity in Christ and then finding, as so many have, that I cannot countenance my own death I must ask the Lord to hammer in the last nail and finish me off. Even in this act of the will, even in the asking, it is God who works in us to have the willingness to say yes to him and pray for the crucified life to become our day-by-day reality.

There is a mystery to be learned in the conforming of our will to that of the Father. Every child of God must, at last, come to the place where on bended knee he cries out to his Abba Father, perhaps in tears of agony, "Not my will, but Yours." The mystery in this truth is that the path of every believer is as individual as his own identity. One might ask why the Father does not exercise His mighty power, for nothing is impossible for Him, to immediately conform every child of His to His perfect will. There are many who have learned of the crucified life and long to enter into it and prayed unsuccessfully for the Lord to bring it about. God's timing is always perfect and rarely is it consistent with ours. His methods are infinitely varied and apparently aimed at the need of every heart. He acted in the most drastic manner possible with Job to bring him to repentance and the surrender of his will. The Psalmist declares:

> The sacrifices of God are a broken spirit, a broken and contrite heart, O God, you will not despise. Psalm 51:17

It seems that this is the very sacrifice that God seeks from all of us and no one can predict what that breaking point will be. For Peter it was when the cock crowed at his third denial of the Lord. For Paul it was immediate and dramatic, not a slow lifelong turnaround but an encounter on the Damascus road that broke a will radically opposed to the Lord.

> "Saul, why are you persecuting me? It is hard for you to kick against the goads. Acts 26:14

Though Paul's transformation was singular his practice of "kicking against the goads" is not. Many of God's children battle against the call to the crucified life. The self-will does not go easily and it is only when we acknowledge our helplessness before it that we cry out to God. Your self was crucified with Christ. The self died and we are called to reckon ourselves dead, not pretend, but accept by faith what has actually already taken place. Our fear of the cross is misplaced. Christ endured the sufferings of the cross in our place and offers in exchange for our self-life his resurrection life. He calls us in Matthew 11 to take up his yoke.

> Come to me all you are weary and burdened, and I will give you rest. Take my yoke upon you and learn from me, for I am gentle and humble in heart and you will find rest for your souls. For my yoke is easy and my burden is light. Matthew 11:28-30

The crucified life has also been called the exchanged life. Christ calls us to exchange our failed efforts, which are a heavy burden beyond bearing, for his yoke, which is a yoke of rest, one that is light. This is mysterious to us. How can our death lead to rest? The answer is that Christ does all the work. We need only choose to walk with Him. This picture would have been well understood to the agricultural mind of Jesus' day. It was customary to train a young ox by yoking him to an older experienced ox. The older ox bore the weight of plowing. The younger simply walked beside Him learning to trust the yoke and to plow straight in obedience to the plowman. Christ is the experienced ox who does all the work if we choose not to go our own way and not to let our crucified self retain control of our life's direction.

Not only is the crucified life one of rest it is one of inexpressible joy according to

Peter.

> In this you greatly rejoice, though now for a little while you may have had to suffer grief in all kinds of trials. These have come so that your faith – of greater worth than gold, which perishes even though refined by fire – may prove genuine and may result in praise, glory and honor when Jesus Christ is revealed. Though you have not seen Him you love Him; and even though you do not see Him now, you believe in Him and are filled with inexpressible joy…1 Peter 1:6-8

Only in Christ can we link together the experiences of suffering and joy. As the writer to the Hebrews says, those who have entered into His rest have ceased from their own labors. (Hebrews 4:10) Once one discovers that he no longer has to work for his salvation and that he neither has to work for his own perfection it is indeed a joy inexpressible. This is the treasure, the pearl of great price, to be discovered by every believer – Christ in us the hope of glory – Christ living His supernatural overcoming life in us and through us. All that it requires is that we acknowledge our death on the cross with Him in order that we may know and experience that same life and power that raised Him from the dead.

> "The cross is no longer a cross when there is no self to suffer under it." [5]

Chapter Six

---

[5] Francis Fenelon, The Best of Fenelon (Gainesville: Bridge/Logos, 2002).

The Spirit of Prayer

How does our understanding that our bodies are God's temples affect the call to pray? When Jesus cleansed the temple He declared My house shall be a house of prayer. "'It is written', he said to them, "'My house will be called a house of prayer,' but you are making it a 'den of robbers.'" (Matthew 21:13) We have already pointed to Hebrews to explain that the Jerusalem temple was always a shadow of the true temple in heaven and the one to come in which the Spirit of God permanently dwells – the Church. As living stones in the spiritual temple Peter teaches that every believer is a temple. If this is true then it follows that God's desire is that our newly created temples also should be houses of prayer. We know that when Jesus overturned the tables in the Jerusalem temple it did not result in any change. As He left Jerusalem that day He turned and looking back at the city said:

> "O Jerusalem, Jerusalem, you who kill the prophets and stone those sent to you, how often I have longed to gather your children together, as a hen gathers her chicks under her wings, but you were not willing. Matthew 12:37

The old temple is a symbol of the failure of human effort to win salvation and favor with God. Undoubtedly the overturned tables were back up the next day and the moneychangers renewed their trade. If Jesus could have reformed us by going to work on our old temple he surely would have. The Jerusalem temple was completely destroyed in 70 A.D. thus turning our hopes to the new creation "We live by faith, not by sight" (2 Corinthians 5:17) where the new has come and the old has passed away. Surely His intention for His new temples is that they be houses of prayer. The veil has been torn in two:

> By his death, Jesus opened a new and living way through the curtain into the most holy place. (Hebrews 10:20) NLT

We all individually have full access to the Holy of Holies as a royal priesthood. We can pray continually and know that we shall be heard by virtue of our standing in Christ.

How then do we reconcile this wide open door to the throne room of God and our general ineffectiveness in prayer? Jesus said, "ask and you shall receive." (John 16:24) The question actually is, do we go to the Father with our will or to discover His will? Tozer shed light on this saying:

> "Anything that falls within the circle of His will He gives freely to whosoever asks aright, but not days or weeks of fasting and prayer will persuade Him to alter anything that has come out of His mouth."[6]

Another man of God speaks to this in like manner:

> "We should not behave as if our cry to God is a way of forcing Him to answer." [7]

We long for rules and principles of prayer that will assure us of answers to our

---

[6] A. W. Tozer, Tozer Speaks (Camp Hill: Wingspread Publishers, 1994).

[7] Lefebvre, ibid. 33.

perceived needs little realizing the arrogance and the risk of witchcraft in approaching the Father in this way. Imagine a child trying to tell his father how to manage his household and you'll see in some small way how little regard we have for who God actually is and our true position in His kingdom. It is arrogance that even gives us the idea that we can manipulate God. This was Balaam's error, an error that led to his death.

Only when Balaam forsook his practice of witchcraft did he truly hear God.

> Now when Balaam saw that it pleased the Lord to bless Israel, he did not resort to divination as at other times, but turned his face toward the wilderness. Numbers 24:1

Many Christians believe in divination in their prayer life without realizing it. God was determined to bless Israel and Balaam failed to change His mind. Prayer is never about changing the mind of God. It is about discovering the mind of God. When Balaam "turned his face toward the wilderness" he set aside his own plan and intentions and opened his heart and mind to wait on and hear from God.

We can never know the mind of God apart from entering into a direct relationship with Him. We must steadfastly resist any other strategy but submission and surrender. When the Diaspora Jews wanted an answer for every situation and possibility affecting their relationship with God they developed the Mizvot – 613 laws or rules which, if kept, insured one's good standing with God and thus His favor in prayer. This is and was a patent attempt to move God on the basis of human behavior that men classified by their own reckoning to be righteous. This is the fundamental flaw in every failed prayer life. Christians will fast and pray for days, and even weeks in the vain attempt to achieve an answer to some predetermined request, as though we could change God's mind by somehow putting Him in our debt through self-imposed sacrifice. This is a misunderstanding of fasting and the true spirit of prayer. Prayer is always a matter of seeking and discovering, an activity, which can only succeed if initiated and directed by the Holy Spirit.

Jesus initiated Nicodemas into this mystery in John three. Nicodemas, like any teacher, wished to get to the bottom of knowing God by learning from Jesus some principle or rule. Jesus cautioned him about taking this approach if he wanted to be born again.

> "How can someone be born when they are old?" Nicodemas asked. "Surely they cannot enter a second time into their mother's womb to be born!" Jesus answered, "Very truly I will tell you, no one can enter the kingdom of God unless they are born of water and of the spirit. You should not be surprised at my saying, "You must be born again." The wind blows wherever it pleases. You hear its sound, but you cannot tell where it comes from or where it is going. So it is with everyone born of the spirit." John 3:4-8

He goes on to explain that there must be a clear distinction between earthly and "heavenly things." The heavenly economy operates not just differently from the earthly one but most often in the opposite manner. We cannot relate to God as though He acted and thought as we do.

> "For my thoughts are not your thoughts, neither are your ways my ways," declares the Lord. Isaiah 55:8

These who would learn to pray through trying to figure out God set themselves on a course that never ends. Jesus use of the wind analogy communicates the fundamental unpredictability of the Spirit. Thus He says, "So it is with everyone born of the spirit." Our new life is the life of the Holy Spirit. As Titus 3:5 tells us, "He saved us…by the renewing of the Holy Ghost." Apparently we can't learn the ways of the Spirit. What we must learn is to submit to and be controlled by the Holy Spirit. Any attempt on our part to control the answer to prayer is, in effect, usurping the role of the Spirit.

> "We do not know what we ought to pray for, but the Spirit Himself intercedes for us with groans that words cannot express. And He who searches our hearts knows the mind of the Spirit, because the Spirit intercedes for the saints in according with the will of God." Romans 8:26-27

Thomas Merton said, "We believe, not because we want to know, but because we want to be." (Innocent Bystander). It is our turning to the tree of knowledge that causes us to fail in prayer. We seek knowledge in order to gain power in the hope that we might prevail in prayer. Thus we miss the single most important purpose of prayer – becoming. The will of God, first and foremost, is to transform His children into the image of Christ. We cannot go around the first principle of the will of God to pray otherwise – prayer is about being in a transforming relationship with

God. It is as though just being with Him changes us.

> And we, who with unveiled faces all reflect the Lord's glory, are being transformed into His likeness with everlasting glory, which comes from the Lord, <u>who is the Spirit</u>. 2 Corinthians 3:18

Paul points to the agency of the Holy Spirit in this work, that same One who unpredictably blows about like the wind. What then are we to pray? Antony Bloom speaks of our relational encounters with God as crisis moments. Crisis is derived from the Greek "krisis" which means judgment. Bloom says that every meeting with God involves judgment. Being in the presence of the Spirit of truth always exposes all that is untrue in us. Imagine the light of His glory shining in the hidden and darkened places of our soul exposing and convicting. The Father does this with a humble, gentle love, and never more than we can bear, through the Spirit. Unless we acknowledge this fundamental work as necessary for our spiritual life we will ever approach God in confusion and frustration. This transforming work has a two-fold aim, preparing us for eternity and secondly preparing us for service. Indeed we can most effectively do the work of the King as we become like Him. Thus what God reveals to us about the condition of our own soul becomes that which we pray about, asking God to make the necessary changes and acting out in obedience the steps to be taken. Our God is holy. This means that His standard of truth is absolute and because of this there is no other way we can approach Him but in complete agreement with Him about the condition of our souls.

> If I had cherished sin in my heart, the Lord would not have listened. Psalm 66:18

Christ's sacrifice for our sin paid the full price for all. Unfortunately we tend to embrace a legal understanding of this work and forget that its intention was to bring us into a relationship with God that makes us His children. God has no tolerance for liars and those who practice self-deception. The work of justification begins the work of transformation – a work needed to fit us for an eternity of fellowship with God. We cannot simply take the promises of answered prayer and ignore God's desire for integrity and holiness in His children.

Christ died because of our irreparable brokenness. It is because of this continuing brokenness that we are quite incapable of knowing what is best for us in terms of prayer and still less what is best for others. Therefore we are dependent on God to reveal His will, which we in turn pray for and, if need be, act on. Some might say that the scriptures teach us what to pray. This is certainly true except that the scribes and Pharisees knew the scriptures better than anyone. Yet the Lord said of them:

> You diligently study the scriptures because you think by them you possess eternal life. These are the scriptures that testify about me. John 5:39

Those of us who read the bible before the new birth learned what the Pharisees did not. Apart from the Holy Spirit we are blind and deaf to the truths of scripture. Even the promises of answered prayer and the instructions regarding what to pray in scripture have no power apart from the leading and direction of the Spirit.

All that is humble is prayer, for true prayer humbles us. Prayer is an act of utter dependence on God, an acknowledgement that everything (even what to pray) comes from Him. The basis of this is coming to God as we are and as He is. In fact prayer is seeing ourselves as God sees us. This is only possible in and through the working of the Spirit. He reveals, He teaches, He guides and ultimately He grants us empowering grace to change. Grace is God's gift but it must be sought and received. It is in prayer that we seek God's precious gifts of grace.

Another misunderstanding in prayer is the teaching regarding prayer in Jesus name. Not a few teachers present this as though we were Aladdin standing before the stone blocking the entrance of the cave of the forty thieves. Inside the cave were untold treasures accessible if Aladdin could discover the magic word that opened the doorway to the cave. Jesus' name is not the spiritual equivalent of open sesame. Simply saying "In Jesus Name" has no value at all in gaining the Father's acquiescence to our prayers. This was never Jesus intention in teaching us to pray. He gave multiple exhortations to pray to the Father in His name.

> "And whatsoever ye shall ask in my name, that will I do, that the Father may be glorified in the Son." John 14:13
>
> "You may ask me anything in my name, and I will do it." John 14:14
>
> "You did not choose me, but I chose you and appointed you to go and bear fruit – fruit that will last. Then the Father will give you whatever you ask in my name." John 15:16
>
> "In that day you will no longer ask me anything. I tell you the truth, my Father will give you whatever you ask in my name." John 16:23

> "Until now you have not asked for anything in my name.
> Ask and you will receive, and your joy will be complete."
> John 16:24
>
> "In that day you will ask in my name. I am not saying
> that I will ask the Father on your behalf." John 16:26

We would like to understand this in the open sesame sense but we must not forget that in following Christ we are called to imitate both His relationship with the Father and His character. This means two things that absolutely place limits on what we ask:

1. In coming to the Father in prayer we must never ask for something from the Father that Jesus Himself would not ask.
2. Since Jesus repeatedly declared that He never once acted on His own will but entirely submitted to the will of the Father, then we can and must do no less in prayer.

This is what asking in His name means. If we are to bring the Lord's name to the Father we must never misuse it or misrepresent Him in any way. This brings us back to the need for transformation. It follows that the more we are like our Lord the more we shall prevail in prayer.

Ultimately the practice of prayer is to bring us into the supernatural realm. It does not bring God down to us. It draws us up into Him. The natural realm, as we perceive it, is ruled by natural laws. If we are going to operate outside of or beyond those laws we must begin with the power that Paul spoke of in Ephesians 1:19-20, the power that raised Jesus from the dead which He says is at work in us who believe. We cannot find within our own resources the power to heal the sick, deliver the demonized or raise the dead. It is God who works in and through us. Jesus himself declared that He only did what the Father did, said what the Father said and went where the Father was going. (John 5:19) Everything He did in His ministry was done through His relationship with the Father and in submission to the moment-by-moment revealed will of the Father.

The secret is in waiting on God rather than barging into His presence and boldly telling Him what we want and insisting He accept our analysis of what is best in any given situation. One of the simple truths in our relationship with Him is that He is God and in the most absolute manner possible we are not. How can we ever dare to say to God what needs to be done in any situation? He alone knows everything. Isaiah advises us to wait on God.

> But they who wait for the Lord shall renew their strength; they shall mount up with wings as eagles; they shall run and not be weary; they shall walk and not faint. Isaiah 40:31

The eagle is a perfect picture of a life born up by the wind of the Spirit. The eagle soars, rises and falls on the wings of the wind. It is the strength and power of the Spirit of God in us that carries us beyond our natural abilities and limits. This is a life for those who "wait" on God, for those who are willing to seek Him and to let Him do the work rather than ask Him to bless ours "In Jesus Name." This is why Jesus said "learn of Me" and you will find rest for your souls, for My yoke is easy and My burden is light. (Matthew 11:30) Who can teach us more effectively than the Lord Himself, if we are going to learn how to pray. He will even teach us how to "wait." Prayer is in its simplest understanding a school. We go to prayer in order to know God, know His will and be transformed by it. Ministry is a by-product or, if you will, the fruit, of a deep and abiding life of prayer. We do not go to the Father to get, we go to grow. A true life of intercession actually comes from the heart of God and this takes place when our heart is one with His. We then care about and love what He cares for and loves. This results from being with Him and being transformed by Him. This is what Jesus meant when He spoke of abiding.

> If you abide in me, and my words abide in you, ask whatever you wish, and it will be done for you. John 15:7

The only way to pray in Jesus name is to abide in Him.

Chapter Seven
The Call to Wait

How does a culture, and I mean the culture that exists in the North American church, a culture that is used to a rapid pace of action, slow down and even stop to wait on God? Can we assume that because we have a sense of urgency that our God thinks and acts in like manner? Does He see the world as we do? Is it His purpose to serve our perceived needs and facilitate our plans, even those for evangelism and kingdom building? How do we understand a God for whom a thousand years is but a day, who promised a Messiah to Eve and then took four thousand years to bring it about, who promised Canaan to Abraham and then waited 430 years to give the land to Abraham's descendents. It seems that there is a pattern of waiting on God in the lives of all of the saints through the scriptures. Is our day different? Do we too need to wait on God? The answer is found in the truth that God does not change nor has he ever accommodated Himself to a culture in order to work out His plans and purposes.

A fundamental reality underpins our need to wait on God. Jesus said in John 5:19 that He could do nothing by Himself. If this was true of the sinless Son of God we all need to ask ourselves, what then can I do? We must begin with the sure and certain attitude that we are utterly dependant on God to do anything of value in His kingdom. John One speaks of Jesus as the living Word. The connection to Genesis One is obvious and clearly intended. Jesus is that same Word in creation that brought light and life out of darkness and chaos. Through John the Holy Spirit wants us to understand the necessity of God speaking. It is when God speaks that everything changes. Through speaking He creates and He saves. Through speaking He saves, heals, and delivers. The scriptures, as essential as they are have no power apart from the living will of God in any moment. John affirmed this in His first epistle.

> That which was from the beginning, which we have heard, which we have seen with our eyes, which we have looked at and our hands have touched – this we proclaim concerning the Word of life. 1 John 1:1

John did not proclaim words on a page but a living Word of life – Jesus Christ the Word made flesh.

It is this living Word that we must wait for if we are going to be men and women who prevail in prayer. The New Testament text most often used and misrepresented in teaching us how to pray is James 5.

> The prayer of a righteous person is powerful and effective. Elijah was a human being, even as we are. He prayed earnestly that it would not rain, and it did not rain on the land for three and half years. Again he prayed, and the heavens gave rain, and the earth produced its crops. 5:16-17

A surface reading of this passage leads one to conclude that because of Elijah's personal righteousness God was moved to answer his prayers. A closer look at the actual events reveals something deeper. The story is in 1 Kings 18, and leads to

Elijah's encounter with the prophets of Baal on Mount Carmel. Again it appears that Elijah controlled the rain through his prayers but this was never the case. He was always acting in response to the living word of God.

> After a long time, in the third year, the word of the Lord came to Elijah: "Go and present yourself to Ahab, and I will send rain on the land." 1 Kings 18:1

When Elijah went to Mount Carmel the Lord had already told him it was going to rain. We can infer that it was the Lord who instructed Elijah to pray that it would not rain 3 ½ years previous. This is both a mystery and a clue to the question of prevailing prayer and thus our call to wait on God to speak. For some reason unexplained, God has tied His spoken and revealed will to our prayers. This is illustrated by Elijah's prayer in 18:41-45. Though there wasn't a cloud in sight he told Ahab "there is a sound of heavy rain." He then began to pray. Six times he prayed and nothing happened. The seventh time his servant reported, "a cloud as small as a man's hand is rising from the sea." Then it began to rain. What God had already spoken out Elijah needed to pray for, and his faith and persistence were both tested. He did not stop until what God had said would happen, happened. Thus prayer is a vital link in the chain of fulfilling the will of God. Where did Elijah's righteousness come into this? Firstly, he was a man who sacrificed his whole life in exchange for intimacy with God. He put himself in the place where he could hear God and serve His will. Secondly, he prayed with faith and perseverance even when the answer was not immediate. This, I believe, is the proper way to understand the reference to him in James Five and how we should apply this teaching on prayer to ourselves. We must wait in prayer on God to reveal His will and then we begin to pray for His will to come to pass and persist until it does. Any suggestion, that repeating prayers to the point of irritating Him into giving in, is both ridiculous and an insult to His holiness. This idea is sometimes drawn from the parable of the unjust judge in Luke 18. The point of the parable is not that the widow prevailed by nagging but that God is not at all like the unjust judge. Yes, we are to persist in prayer but not because we think we can force Him to respond but actually as an expression of our belief in His faithfulness. Waiting on God for Him to speak honors His sovereign authority. Waiting on Him to answer is equally a commitment to honoring Him as Lord. Our faith in Him is both pleasing to Him and one of the simplest ways we can express our love for Him. This was the great truth that characterized the life of Abraham.

> ...He did not waver through unbelief regarding the promise of God, but was strengthened in His faith and gave glory to God, being fully persuaded that God had power to do what He had promised. Romans 4:20-21

He was another who understood waiting on God. Knowing the culture of His day it is almost certain that Abraham and Sarah had prayed for many years for a child. Fertility was a sign of God's blessing, barrenness, of his disfavor. Finally God spoke His promise when Abraham was 75.

> The Lord appeared to Abraham and said, "To your offspring I will give this land." Genesis 12:7

What Abraham did not know then was that it would be 25 years before God fulfilled His promise and then only when he and Sarah were beyond the physical possibility of having a child.

> Without weakening in his faith, he faced the fact that his body was as good as dead – since he was about a hundred years old – and that Sarah's womb was also dead. Romans 4:19

Here again we have the same two elements.

1. Waiting for God to speak
2. Waiting for God to answer, both in the context of a prayerful submission to God.

We know that Abraham continued to press the Lord over the next 25 years. Eight years later in Genesis 15 he reminded the Lord of his promise and that he was still seeking its fulfillment.

> "You have given me no children, so a servant in my household will be my heir." Genesis 15:3

God replied by reaffirming what He has already said.

> Then the word of the Lord came to him: "This man will not be your heir." He took him outside and said, "Look up at the heavens and count the stars – if indeed you can count them." Then He said to him, "So shall your offspring be." Abraham believed the Lord, and He credited it to him as righteousness. 15:4-6

The delay and his and Sarah's increasing age raised some real questions that Abraham posed in prayer. God's answer makes it clear that it is not the quality of our prayer that God looks to but our faith in His promise. We are called to hear in prayer the will of God and then to pray it out in faith. The background of both is the necessity of waiting on God.

David was the great teacher of this prayer necessity in the Psalms.

> Be still before the Lord and wait patiently for Him; do not
> fret when men succeed in their ways, when they carry out
> their wicked schemes. Psalm 37:7

The Psalms are liberally weighted with like references to waiting on God. David learned this as both Abraham and Elijah before him. He received a promise from God at the age of 15 or 16 and then waited until he was 30 for the promise to unfold, nine of those years spent fleeing from Saul's murderous intentions. He too believed and refused every opportunity to advance the promise by his own hand as he had the advantage over Saul on two separate occasions. Many of the Psalms appear to be written in the caves and wilderness hiding places during those years. David waited and God blessed him richly with a wonderful intimacy in worship. Abraham was the friend of God. David was the man after God's heart. We see that men who prevailed in prayer with God were men who honored Him by waiting on His will and His timing.

There is a pattern of promise and waiting in the lives of nearly all of the greatest saints but we cannot separate intercessory prayer from worship and our relationship with God. Prayer is first of all about this relationship. We must never see it in a utilitarian way. Talking to God is an incredible privilege and responsibility and yet prayer is, if anything, a response to God, as opposed to a response to our perception of our circumstantial needs. Waiting on Him is an act of worship. We are acknowledging Him as He truly is and as we truly are – utterly dependent and subject to His will alone. We never impose our will on Him simply because He alone is God. David demonstrated this when his illegitimate son by Bathsheba was dying. David immediately set himself to wait on God in fasting and prayer for days hoping that God might speak and rescind His word. The child died and David responded neither with frustration or anger at the failure of his prayers. Indeed his response mystifies his servants.

> "Then David got up from the ground. After he had washed, put on lotions and changed his clothes he went into the house of the Lord and worshipped. 2 Samuel 12:20

Surely David would have wanted God to save the child but David was set on seeking the will of God and when he knew it was settled he accepted it and responded with worship. This is what set him apart as a man after God's heart. He cared more for God than himself and for the will of God than his own will. He was a man who waited on God.

Prayer is a living relationship with God that can only be entered into and sustained on His terms. We might understand this better if we lived under an absolute monarchy. Because our persuasion is democratic it is hard for us to contemplate not having a say in how and when things are done. The subjects of a king understand the need to wait on the king's decisions. Our Lord Jesus Christ is the King of

Kings, our Creator and the Sustainer of all creation. We can only come to Him as He is. There is no alternative.

I find any dispensational approach to this teaching fundamentally unbiblical. There is nothing in scripture consistent with the view that God has changed under the terms of the New Covenant. John's encounter with the exalted Lord in Revelations One is entirely in agreement with the descriptions of Isaiah, Daniel, and Ezekiel in the presence of God. Nonetheless the pattern of promise, waiting in prayer and fulfillment is seen in the single most important work of the Lord in the foundation of the church. He spent 40 days with his disciples after his resurrection instructing them about the kingdom of God and then spoke of a promise they were to wait in prayer for.

> Do not leave Jerusalem, but wait for the gift my Father promised, which you have heard me speak about. For John baptized with water, but in a few days you will be baptized with the Holy Spirit. Acts 1:4

Following his departure the disciples began the most famous prayer meeting in the history of the Church.

> When they arrived they went upstairs to the room where they were staying… they all joined together constantly in prayer, along with the woman and Mary the mother of Jesus, and with His brothers. Acts 1:13-14

They waited as the Lord commanded and after 10 days the promise was fulfilled.

What if they had proceeded in haste after His departure to prosecute the Great Commission? After all, His last words in Matthew 28 called them to go into all the world to make disciples. They would have been obedient and certainly pursuing a kingdom priority. One wonders how many Christians have never waited on God but simply taken the commands in His word and ministered the gospel without the power and the living Word of the King. Waiting is time consuming. Time spent in prayer seems to be unproductive and especially in our day, time poorly spent. But it was with the power and blessing of the Lord that those same disciples who waited saw 3000 conversions in one day and then 5000 more only a few days later. It is no coincidence that Peter and John were going to the temple at the hour of prayer. They had learned that true effectiveness lies in waiting on God in prayer.

One of the great challenges of our time is practicing silence. Everyone, it seems, has a cell phone, IPod or a television on wherever they go. It is almost as though we avoid silence and yet waiting on God is all about listening. How can we hear God if we do not listen? How can we listen if we continuously avoid silence? This must become the practice of every Christian who wishes to prevail in prayer. Our discomfort with silence must be dealt with or we will be ill equipped to wait on God. In our next chapter we will deal with our fear of silence in the presence of God.

Chapter Eight
The Grace of God

The role of grace in entering into intimacy with God cannot be underestimated. Paul teaches that we are saved absolutely by grace, saying it is a gift of God not of works. (Ephesians 2:8-9) Since we have been saved by grace, does it make any sense that a Christian would attempt to return to a means of walking with God that utterly failed and necessitated the sacrifice of Christ? We are completely unable to live this life by the strength of our own efforts. Paul said to the Galatians, who had forsaken grace and returned to human effort, "Who has bewitched you?" (Galatians 3:1) as if to say that such an approach could only come from a powerful deception.

It is true that a great mystery attends the question of the sovereignty of God and how it interacts with our free will. Every new Christian wishes to honestly respond to what they believe is their responsibility in growing in Christ and coming into spiritual maturity. This is where the problem of receiving grace is manifested. After a life, prior to conversion, of being entirely in control, our habitual response is to retain at least a measure of control, to help God in the process of sanctification. This is done with the very best of motives, even a passion rooted in love for God. We want to demonstrate our gratitude for His saving us by obedience. The mystery is that this actually hinders grace. Grace is not something given to us to use. It is God himself at work in us. We would like to see God as a sort of battery charging station to which we come when our power is low. We simply charge ourselves up and then go and live. What we do not see is that even if this were true we are fundamentally incompetent and incapable of properly using and exercising such power. God does not give grace for us to use. He retains it for Himself to work as

He sees fit in us and through us. Our responsibility is to prayerfully seek the working of grace and thereby become receptive to God's work.

The grace and love of God can only be understood and received in the context of a deep and abiding conviction of sin. Many Christians have never known this and thus have no grasp of how much God loves them. This causes Christians to work for the Father's approval.

All of the life of a Christian is to be a response to God's love. Paul declared that God's strength is made perfect in our weakness. Our reluctance to accept this weakness militates against God's work in us. Militate may seem to be a strong word but it reflects the truth that our old nature is at war with the new. Jesus said in the Sermon on the Mount that the meek would inherit the earth. His first beatitude declaration was that the poor in spirit are blessed. He meant that those who recognize their spiritual poverty are blessed. It is therefore a blessing to be weak and to willingly accept this as your condition since His strength is revealed in our weakness. Failure to humbly accept our own weak condition actually causes God to resist our efforts.

> God opposes the proud but gives grace to the humble. 1 Peter 5:5

Though our motives are good in our minds any attempt to do the work of the kingdom or to grow in the knowledge of God will never succeed apart from our absolute dependence on God.

Jesus began His incarnation by laying aside all of His own power and will and by committing to accept without question the Father's agenda and the Spirit's empowering. Only those who do likewise can follow Him in a relationship with the Father and in ministry. Jesus said during his garden arrest that He could have called on 10,000 angels to rescue Him if He wished. His poverty was intentional. Ours is very real, just not perceived. This is why Jesus said it is hard for a rich man to enter into the kingdom. Those who think they are rich or strong are either unwilling or unable to receive the riches of the kingdom or the strength of God. The belief that we need to be somehow self-sufficient is misplaced. Our poverty and utter dependence on the Father arouses His loving compassion. Self-sufficiency produces the opposite. God resists the proud.

We simply need contrast the healing of blind Bartimaeus with Jesus' words to the Pharisees.

> Jesus said, "For judgment I have come into this world, so that the blind will see and those who see will become blind." Some Pharisees who were with Him heard him say this and asked, "What, are we blind too?" Jesus said, "If you were blind you would not be guilty of sin; but now that you claim you can see, your sin remains." (John 9:39-41)

In Mark 10 blind Bartimaeus loudly called out to Jesus and would not be restrained by those around him. Remarkably Jesus asks him what he wants.

> "What do you want me to do for you?" Jesus asked him.
> The blind man said, "Rabbi, I want to see."

This illustrates the very principle the Lord wants us to understand in our approach to Him. The Pharisees could not see because they were unwilling to acknowledge their spiritual blindness. Bartimaeus pursued the Lord in full recognition of his need and his blindness was healed. The Lord even sought from him confession of that need before he healed him. This is how God's grace works. He resists those who are unwilling to acknowledge their need and pours out His grace on those who humbly bring their need to Him.

Simone Weil had a gift for connecting suffering with the experience of grace. She took a very provocative position on evil by saying that evil is not actually evil but a means of grace in our lives.

> "Duty is given to us in order to kill the self…we only attain to real prayer after we have worn down our own will by keeping rules." [8]

This is the seventh chapter of Romans and the lesson of Moses' law rolled up into one idea. From the moment Adam's heart separated and became "self-sufficient" apart from God He gradually and then more quickly lost his grasp of holiness and truth. Law emerged to cover this deficit. What should have been written on men's hearts was written down so they would know God's will. This was made necessary by increasing lawlessness. What also emerges was what Paul described in Romans seven, man's endless inability to exercise His will in keeping the law. In Galatians 3:24-25 Paul describes the law as "our schoolmaster to lead us unto Christ." By our failure to keep it we realize the utter incompetence of the most zealous and

---

[8] Weill. Ibid. xxxvi.

determined will and we become open to the need of grace, which comes through Christ alone. Christians accept this principle up to the point of salvation but we are quick to abandon it as a fundamental principle of growth in sanctification and maturity in the image of Christ. We never lose our complete need of grace, which can only be received in recognition of that need as an absolute.

This is why Weil speaks of the necessity of pain and suffering. Any attempt to shield ourselves from it also shields us from the lesson it might teach us about our need for God. This is what she means when she says that evil isn't necessarily evil. Its presence and action can lead us to the grace of God and an ever-deepening dependence on Him. Failure is a wonderful teacher and, depending on our degree of pride and self-reliance, an utterly necessary one.

The beauty of grace is that it releases us from the cycle of failure and recommitment to do better. As our Creator and Redeemer only God can do the work of transforming a heart that Jeremiah speaks of in the clearest terms.

> The heart is deceitful above all things and beyond cure.
> Who can understand it? (17:9)

Not only is the human heart beyond cure, it is beyond our ability to even understand. When we accept what the theologians describe as _total_ depravity we can abandon any thought of trying to do the impossible and surrender to the work of God.

The greatest difficulty in understanding and accepting this is our desire to clearly spell out our responsibility in our relationship with God. This leads to what has been described as "too many cooks in the kitchen." God, neither wants, nor does He need our suggestions or advice. He wants a clear field for Him to work unhindered by our interference or resistance. All He asks of us is faith. Trust in His promise that He will finish what He started, what He has predestined to take place?

> For those God foreknew he also predestined to be conformed to the likeness of his Son, that he might be the firstborn among many brothers. Romans 8:29

Grace operates most effectively in acknowledged weakness and faith. Abraham modeled this faith in waiting for a promised heir and the promise was fulfilled when his and Sarah's weakness was absolute.

We must never forget that God defines grace as a gift. A gift is simply received. It is hard for us to comprehend the infinite and unfailing love of God, which never requires performance for it to be conferred. God is delighted by our trust in His love and our willing reception of it.

Some might object to this as cheap grace. Where are the works? Where is the holiness and the obedience? The answer lies in our acceptance of grace and the humbling of our hearts.

> The sacrifices of God are a broken spirit; a broken and contrite heart, O God, you will not despise. Psalm 51:17

The foundation of Christ's saving work is man's incompetence and the depravity of our fallen heart. We should begin the Christian life with humility in the face of our fallen condition and need for a Savior. But our hearts deceive us. What we freely received as a gift of grace soon becomes the pursuit of holiness and obedience in our own strength. The journey of many believers is often down one of the pilgrim's (progress) side roads into a prison of our own choosing. We learn with great difficulty that first lesson of salvation once again – not by works of righteousness, which we have done. Grace saved us and only by grace can we become holy and live a life of obedience.

After three years of being with Jesus Peter believed with self-assurance that he would never deny the Lord. Indeed he would follow Him to the death. We know that when the test came he failed absolutely. His dependence on his own self-sufficiency not only betrayed the Lord but also revealed to him his own heart and in that moment his pride was broken. The Lord reminded him of his three-fold denial in John 21 by asking him to declare his love three times. Jesus intended to restore him to apostolic leadership but with the understanding that he should never forget the lesson of trusting in his own heart. It is not surprising that it was Peter who taught that God resists the proud but gives grace to the humble.

It is God who works in us to will to do His good pleasure. Grace is so deeply rooted in our relationship with God that even the will to do good is a product of grace at work in us. It only follows that the good works themselves are also the result of grace. We can take credit for nothing as much as we would like to. Left to ourselves we would be like the dog that returns to his vomit. Is this a form of hyper-Calvinism? Not at all. We have one work, which the history of saints before us has taught us pleases God. It is the work of faith, believing God. Trusting God honors Him and is the highest form of worship available to us. It is this trust that elicits the abundant grace of God.

In its simplest terms, what is grace? The danger in trying to get a handle on grace is found in de-personalizing it. Grace has an aspect of power to it but to understand it as something like gasoline or electricity is utterly insulting to the holiness and love of God. Grace has everything to do with becoming like Christ, the maturing and transforming work of the Holy Spirit. We must see ourselves as babies growing and the role of God is to parent us. Growth is natural but it requires nutrition. That which gives us the ability to grow is the very person of Christ in us as we are shaped and directed through the agency of the Holy Spirit. It might even be helpful to think of our newborn life as a baby in a nursery being fathered by God the Father and mothered by Holy Spirit. This whole process of growing is the work of grace in us. We confuse the notion of power to do ministry with grace. This isn't helpful at all and actually is a distortion of God's work. Grace is intended to make us like Christ in His holiness and His character. Fruit in our relationship with God and in ministry is the result.

The analogy given by the Lord about gardening, in John 15, helps us to see this. Abiding in Him leads to fruit. It isn't just the flow of life-giving sap but the abiding connection to Christ Himself that produces the fruit. The identity of the tree determines the resulting fruit. Grace isn't just the power of Christ in us. It is the person of Christ in us. When Jesus said in John 14:6 "I am the way, the truth and the life" He was not making a doctrinal or analogous statement. He was speaking literally with emphasis on the "I." He himself is each and every one of these things. We don't just need the work of grace in us. It is the very reason for our existence. Christ redeemed us to restore us into the image of God and into union and communion with the Father. As grace works in us we are changed and the result of these changes is spiritual fruit.

Our role is to receive grace. Our great obstacle to this is pride and self-sufficiency. Humility is the doorway to grace and fellowship with the one who works grace in us. Scripture is clear on this:

1. Isaiah 66:1-2 – God esteems the humble and contrite.
2. 1 Peter 5:5-7 – God gives grace to the humble.
3. Isaiah 57:15 – God dwells with the humble.
4. James 4:10 – God lifts up the humble.
5. Psalm 51:17 – God accepts the sacrifice of the humble.

To even enter into the mystery of grace one needs to recognize his need, rooted in a never-ending dependence on God. Grace is entirely free. Any notion of working for it denies that grace is entirely gratuitous. God will not give grace as a reward. It arises absolutely out of His love for us. Thus the path to the fullness of grace is trustful submission on God's terms. Determine that you will remain (abide) humbly in God's hands and let Him do with you all that He pleases. Patience, humility and faith will lead to an abundant experience of the grace of God. This begins with the end of self.

Chapter Nine
The End of Self

Our reactions to scriptural calls to self-denial are colored with images of monks and nuns in monasteries and penitent worshippers flagellating themselves while climbing the steps of cathedrals on bloodied knees. These behaviors are actually carnal applications of a spiritual truth which strengthen the influence and power of the self-life. Denial of self can mistakenly be taken for gaining grace through sacrifice. Self-imposed suffering is just that – <u>self</u>-imposed. The self-denial of Christ was in obedience to the will of the Father. Jesus, in fact, as a part of that obedience, gave up any self-directed or self-imposed activity in fulfilling the Father's will. His obedience was total. This is why He is our model in practicing self-denial. We cannot pick and choose from a spiritual menu as though we were standing before a salad bar. The surrender of our self-life must be so complete that everything flows from the Father, and that He alone determines our choices.

If we understand self-denial as a sacrificial means of gaining God's grace and favor we deny the fundamental principle of grace. We are saved and sanctified by the free grace of God – not of works lest any man should boast. (Ephesians 2:9) The question of our role in both naturally breeds confusion and may lead to rejection of the teaching in scripture on self-denial. This is a tragedy for anyone who casts aside self-denial because this teaching can be an incredibly wonderful source of joy for those who understand it properly. The difficulty with grace is our inability and sometimes unwillingness to accept its unlimited scope. The desire to add to it arises from misplaced guilt and self-judgment that is difficult to let go of. God's unconditional love is just that. It has no conditions. Our full acceptance is in Christ. When the Father said this is My beloved Son with Whom I am well pleased, Jesus' standing in the Father's love became ours. We who are "in Christ" are accepted in the beloved – the beloved being Christ. This is the essence of the good news. We no longer need to strive for the approval of God the Father. His acceptance is absolute. There is no condemnation to those who are in Christ Jesus. (Romans 8:1) It is the acceptance of the full and complete work of Christ on the cross that is hard for us to process and thus we continue to strive and fail to experience the rest the Lord promised. He who has ceased from his own labors enters into God's rest. (Hebrews 3) It is our experience with the ongoing presence of the self-life that breeds this confusion about grace. Paul tells us that we are crucified with Christ.

> I have been crucified with Christ and I no longer live, but Christ lives in me. The life I live in the body, I live by faith in the Son of God, who loved me and gave himself for me. (Galatians 2:20)

Paul is speaking of the old man, the self-life. We are new creatures in Christ. "We live by faith, not by sight." (2 Corinthians 5:7) and yet we are deeply aware of the ongoing activity of the old self. Paul's exhortations to put off the old and put on the new self created in Christ (Ephesians 4:22-24) can add to the frustration of believers who desire to obey this command but find that it is easier to say than do. The self-life is persistent and it contributes to a sense of failure and guilt that drives some Christians to compensate by performance. In doing so they separate themselves from the very grace necessary to bring the self-life to an end. Paul challenged the Galatians for leaving grace behind and returning to salvation by works. We agree with his assessment of the Galatians as foolish little realizing that the Galatian error, though not as obvious as their return to Judaism, is a common Christian experience. We are all in a battle with the self-life and because it is so close to who we are and who we were before Christ, it is the single greatest enemy we will face in this life. James gets at this truth in his epistle.

> When tempted, no one should say, "God is tempting me." For God cannot be tempted by evil, nor does he tempt anyone; but each person is tempted, when they are dragged away by their own evil desire. James 1:13-14 (NIV)

The same could be said for Satan or the demons. We could blame the devil for tempting us and drawing us into sin, but James is saying that the susceptibility to temptation lies within us. If it were not within us there would be nothing that the devil might offer that would have any power over us. It is this seemingly powerful vestige of the pre-new birth life that Paul calls the self-life, the old man. Its presence is the source of much of our suffering as Christians and the focus of a host of often unanswered questions.

The term self-denial is misleading. It suggests that this is done by our own agency – self denying self. If this were the case then the very part of us that must be dealt with would actually be strengthened. The problem of the self-life is its continuing desire for control and reinforcement. Self takes pride in its victories and desires its own glory, which rightfully belongs to God alone. If we are going to become like Christ self has to be dealt a finishing blow. This can only be done by the Lord through the agency of the indwelling Spirit. This is a work of grace but, as Paul declares in Ephesians Two, grace is a gift and a gift must be received. This requires both submission and obedience. A modern parallel might be the patient putting himself into the hands of a surgeon. The patient cannot operate on himself because of the physical impossibility of him doing so and even if it were he would not have the required skill. Scripture makes this principle clear in both the old and new covenants. Circumcision would have been performed by another on those entering the old covenant. The new was made on the cross and we have already spoken of Christ submitting Himself to a death that could only be executed by others. We who follow Christ by taking up our cross do so with the implied understanding that death to self can only be completed by the work of another. Any attempt on our part to put self to death would be vain and done in fundamental incompetence. One mystic has said that if the knife were in our hands we would do all to minimize the pain. Where it hurts the most is likely the place that requires the work to be done. We cannot be trusted with the death of the self-life simply because our perspective is soaked in self-interest and selfishness. God in His loving grace has committed Himself to this work having promised or, as Romans 8 declares, predestined us to be transformed into the image of Christ. He is infinitely humble and selfless and, if we are to become like Him, there can be no other intention but the end of self.

> "Humility is the displacement of self by the enthronement of God." [9]
>
> "When we no longer find self within our hearts it is because God is present." [10]

---

[9] Andrew Murray, Humility (Minneapolis: Bethany House, 2001).

[10] Georges Lefebvre, The Well-Springs of Prayer (New York: Desclee Company, 1961), 41.

When Paul exhorted the Ephesians to be filled with the Spirit (5:18) he was using an image that is consistent throughout scripture as an expression of a mature relationship with God. True maturity for the believer is being filled to the measure of all the fullness of Christ. (Ephesians 4:11-13) Filling implies emptying in order to make room for that which is poured in. In the case of the end of self, the expression pejoratively applied to some, "he's full of himself" exemplifies the obstacle we face in coming to maturity. If Christ is going to dwell in us in <u>all</u> His fullness we need to get out of the way for Him to take His place on the throne of our lives.

One of the first places in scripture this image is used is Jeremiah 2:13.

> My people have committed two sins: they have forsaken me, the spring of living water and have dug their own cisterns, broken cisterns that cannot hold water.

Blaise Pascal was not the first to speak of the empty vessel inside of us made for and longing to be filled with God. As Jeremiah implies, apart from God, this vessel is broken and incapable of containing the fullness of the Godhead. The new birth recreates us and makes us into a vessel both designed and fit for the indwelling presence. Do you not know that you are the temple of God and that the Spirit of God dwells in you? (1 Corinthians 3:16) The old man, the self is the broken cistern of the old life. It too longs to be filled with that which pleases it and satisfies its lusts. The self desires the things of the world and is driven by and for them, the lust of the flesh, the lust of the eyes and the pride of life – all that is not of God. (1 John 2:15, 16) At the same time the new creation longs for the things of God and for God Himself. The two are at war. Every believer knows this battle and its seemingly endless frustrations and failures. "The good that I would I do not and the evil I would not that I do." (Romans 7) Paul goes on to ask, "Who shall deliver me from this body of death?" His answer "Thanks be to God through Jesus Christ." Christ wins on the cross for us the new life and then works in us through Holy Spirit to change us and free us from our bondage to the old life.

The mystery that eludes many Christians is the purpose of God in leaving us with, what in our experience is, a great liability and hindrance in serving Him and walking in fellowship with Him. Simone Weill says:

> "He emptied Himself of His divinity. We should empty ourselves of the false divinity with which we were born."[11]

It is this sense of false divinity that can only be dealt with by our willing choice to relinquish it. There can only be one God as the first commandment declares and the essence of man's rejection of God is rooted in his desire to be God. These were the very words of the serpent to Eve," You will be like God knowing good and evil. (Genesis 3:5) Once born in this condition we know no other way of looking at the universe we live in. We see ourselves as the masters of our destiny putting our awareness fundamentally outside of the true reality of creation under the sovereignty of God. Conversion opens our eyes to the truth but we are hard pressed when it comes to convincing us of the depth of it – total depravity, total incompetence, almost total ignorance and because of our condition, absolute dependence on God. There is no place for the self life in the economy of the kingdom of God. Realizing and accepting our condition is the first step in detaching us from a self that is incompetent and compulsively set on death. Self is so completely set on retaining

---
[11] Weil. Ibid, 34.

control that it will even take us to hell to retain it. Augustine expressed this truth when he said, "Let me know myself that I may know you." He understood that a lucid and undeniable apprehension of ourselves is the beginning of the true knowledge of God. When we are utterly convinced we are not God we accept the one and only God just as He is.

A.W. Tozer put this truth in the perspective of our destiny and the meaning of our ongoing experience as new children of God.

> "What we need to emphasize is that God has saved us to make us like his Son. His purpose is to catch us on our wild race to hell, turn us around because He knows us, bring judgment on the old self and then create a new self within us, which is Jesus Christ." [12]

As already stated there is and can only be one God. Because the self is obsessed with being God, it must be "judged" before we enter into an eternity of fellowship with God. God is selfless. The realm of the Spirit is not the realm of self but of others. It is not a place for self-seeking. In that realm we cannot commune with God in loving Him and receiving His love, if any vestige of self-love remains. This is the genius of God's plan of salvation. We are born anew by the resurrection life of Christ, the very Spirit of God. We have the DNA of Christ in us and at the same time we are "in" Christ. In Him we are being changed to become humble and selfless and loving just like Him that we may also come to the Father in loving fellowship. The Father's love for Jesus now belongs to us. In dealing with the self-life the Father works not out of a desire to punish or inflict unnecessary pain on us,

---

[12] A. W. Tozer, The Crucified Life (Ventura: Regal, 2011), 164-5.

but out of His loving desire to enable us to both receive His love and return it back to Him.

This returns us to the question of the ongoing presence of the self-life after salvation. Why are we, as the hymnist wrote, "prone to wander, Lord, I feel it, prone to leave the God I love."? As stated the lesson of dependence on God is a difficult one and for most of us we learn this conviction by repeated failure. It is by the failure of self-effort that we become convinced of our need for the grace of God. Only by grace can we be transformed. This means that the entire process of sanctification both in timing and in means must belong to God. When we interfere out of unwillingness to believe in and trust God, we make the work more difficult for ourselves and may even bring about delay. One of the mysteries of this process is that the Father will even pull back grace in order to expose weakness.

This becomes necessary for those who struggle with religious notions about the Christian life. Religious Christians believe in performance and tend to emphasize outward behavior over real inward transformation. This leads to a pattern of suppression of sinful tendencies and actions. There is nothing wrong with this if it is done with a right heart but sometimes religious people are unwilling to even admit to themselves their fundamental sinfulness and take upon themselves the role of maintaining what they believe is an appropriate outward level of Christian behavior. They refuse to accept their need for grace or are confused about the fullness of God's love and acceptance. They live a lie; actually deceiving themselves into thinking that even God does not see their spiritual condition. In most cases the only way that God can breach this wall of self-deception is failure.

This gives perspective to the role of suffering in the lives of Christians. The prevailing illusion that God's first priority for His children is to prosper them in every aspect of their lives makes no room for the clear teaching on suffering in the writings of every New Testament author.

> Consider it pure joy my brothers when you face trials of many kinds because you know that the testing of your faith develops perseverance. Perseverance must finish its work so that you may be mature and complete, not lacking anything. James 1:2-4

We tend to link suffering to persecution for the sake of preaching the gospel. James speaks of "trials of many kinds" and makes a direct link between suffering and the maturing process. Peter makes the same argument in His first epistle. (1:39) Because of the nature of the self-life's resistance to the transforming work of grace it appears that "trials of many kinds" are both necessary and even primary in God's working in us. As difficult for Christians to embrace this perspective it must be seen in the context of eternity. This world and everything in it will pass away in favor of a new heavens and a new earth. God is not invested in making us happy and prosperous in this world but in preparing us for the next. Seventy or eighty years here mean little when we think of eternity. Indeed because our time here is so short God will waste none of it as He does all that is needed to bring us to maturity in Christ. Paul embraced this in his life.

> But whatever was to my profit I now consider loss for the sake of Christ. What is more, I consider everything a loss compared to the surpassing greatness of knowing Christ Jesus my Lord, for whose sake I have lost all things. I

> consider them rubbish that I may gain Christ. Philippians 3:7-8
>
> I press on toward the goal to win the prize for which God has called me heavenward in Christ. Philippians 3:14

Peter echoes Pauls' Philippians Two call to have the same mind as Christ by saying "Arm yourselves also with the same attitude because he who has suffered in his body is done with sin." (1 Peter 4:1) Suffering must never be seen as a means of earning grace. The practices of fasting and chastity have been much misrepresented both by some who apply it and those who criticize what they deem unnecessary self-denial. They are best understood as sacraments in that they are physical symbols of a spiritual reality. Fasting in the physical realm represents the emptying of self in exchange for the fullness of Christ. He who is chaste may appear to be giving up one of life's joys but chastity in its proper understanding is to make room for Christ as your companion. Both are exchanges where what one gives up does not even begin to compare with what is received in exchange. This is the paradigm for all self-denial and the end of self. Why would we hold on to the old self which is set on death and keeping us from the joys of intimacy with God? What self wants to hold onto is ashes when God wants to give us beauty. Self is a cancer that kills but God graciously and lovingly will deal with it. In light of what Christ gave for us what are we willing to give to Him? Does my self have rights as is so often trumpeted in our culture of self-absorption? Do I have a right to comfort, to a home, a wife and children, physical safety, friendship? Christ had none of these. But like him I do have the right to dwell in the heart of God. A right to myself? No, but, I do have a right to Christ.

> I tell you the truth, unless a kernel of wheat falls to the

ground and dies, it remains only a single seed, but if it dies it produces many seeds. The man who loves his life will lose it, while the man who hates his life in this world will keep it for eternal life. John 12:24-25

Chapter Ten
The Love of God

John has sometimes been called the apostle of love. He was the only disciple who recorded the standard by which the world should identify followers of Christ.

> By this all men will know you are my disciples if you love one another. John 13:35

This is the theme of his first epistle in which he makes strong statements about love as the evidence by which one separates true disciples from false.

> God is love. Whoever lives in love lives in God and God in him. 1 John 4:16
>
> If anyone says, "I love God," yet hates his brother, he is a liar. For anyone who does not love his brother, whom he has seen, cannot love God whom he has not seen. 1 John 4:20

Though John speaks of love as a behavior with identifiable fruit, the key to understanding love is in his statement that "God is love." From our limited human perspective, the limit being our fallen nature, we are inclined to see love in terms of definable behaviors or non-behaviors. It is love to give a homeless man shoes on a cold winters night in New York City as a police officer recently did? This action was trumpeted in the news worldwide as an example of an act of love. Whether it be helping the poor or forgiving a painful offense we believe we know what constitutes love. When John says that God is love he is not describing what God does he is telling us who God is. The very essence of God's being is love. It is not an adjectival reference to one of His many activities. It is the source of everything He is and does. When Jesus looks with compassion on the multitudes and feeds the five thousand we are seeing God's love in action. When God sends Israel into Canaan to conquer and destroy all of its inhabitants we are again seeing God's love in action. Because God is love it is impossible for Him to do anything out of any other motivation. We understand behaviors as love from a very finite perspective but also out of our fallen brokenness and separation from God. We can only know what love is through union with Him who is love.

The single greatest barrier between Christians and knowing the love of God is fear. The work of Christ on the cross has fully removed the power of sin and God declares us as "accepted in the beloved." There is no reason for any believer to fear the presence of God. But there remains in all of us a remnant of Adam and Eve's desire to hide from God after their willful rebellion against His word. We know that "God so loved the world (us)" but we have great difficulty comprehending and accepting the Father's unconditional love. The Spirit of God in us makes us deeply aware of sin and the presence of the old self-life. And so we struggle with our ongoing failure to be perfect. The world we live in is based on performance. The place we have in the kingdom, one that is both already and not yet, is solely based on the performance of the Lord Jesus Christ. We can add nothing to His work and are fundamentally incapable of doing so anyway. We should not see our weakness and failure as the enemy of God's love but the cause of it. Our poverty stirs God's love and should continually remind us of it. Paul said that God's strength is perfected in our weakness. One could say that so also is God's love. Yet it is this very weakness in us that causes us to be afraid. John's answer to this was that "perfect love casts out fear." (1 John 4:18) It is the utter perfection of God's love that eludes us. For this reason Paul prays that the Ephesians might "have power, with all the saints, to grasp how long and high and wide is the love of Christ," (Ephesians 3:18) even though this love "surpasses knowledge." (4:19) By this Paul is saying that the love of God is beyond the ability of our minds to know because God is love and God is infinite and eternal. Thus His love is infinite and eternal, far beyond our finite minds. Does this mean that our task is beyond us? Not at all! Solomon gives us the key when he says:

> He (God) has made everything beautiful in it time. He has also set eternity in the hearts of men, ... (Ecclesiastes 3:11)

We can only know the love of God, and by this we mean God Himself, through the heart. In the heart lies this capacity. It is our rational minds that betray us by telling us that an unconditional unfailing love makes no sense at all. There must be a catch. How could God love a creature in all its sinfulness, such as I? In matters of doctrine our minds can serve us well but in the matter of knowing God only our hearts will do. If it were any other way only the wise and the educated could know God. We all have a heart that was made for knowing and loving God.

It is the perfect love of God that is the answer to all of our anxiety and fear. His love releases us to rest in the fullness of his peace and joy. Believing in His love is to complete our surrender to His sovereignty over our lives. We move from believing that we are as we see ourselves to we are as God sees us. We must give up the standards of this world for those of the kingdom. Lefebvre said:

> "We do not give ourselves to Him. We come to realize we are wholly His."[13]

God has already settled our place in His kingdom. He loves us unconditionally and we belong irretrievably to Him. We must come to believe and accept what is already reality.

> Do not be terrified; do not be discouraged, for the Lord your God will be with you wherever you go. Joshua 1:9
> I give them eternal life, and they shall never perish, no one can snatch them out of my hand. John 10:28
> Never will I leave you; never will I forsake you. Hebrews 13:5

How does one accept something that even scripture declares is beyond understanding? There is only one answer – one must experience it. Is this possible? Apparently Paul knew this love which passes understanding. In addressing the Philippians He was able to say:

> "My deep feeling for you comes from the heart of Christ himself." Philippians 1:8

Paul spoke of the substance of his deep feeling of love for the Philippians as from Christ himself. There is nothing mysterious about this if we understand that the work of the cross hasn't just cancelled sin but it has made us literally one with Christ. Paul repeatedly speaks of Christians as dwelling "in Christ." It is through

---

[13] Lefebvre, Well-Springs, 66.

our union with Him that we enter into the Trinitarian communion of the three Persons of the godhead. We receive "in" Christ the Father's love for the Son and the Holy Spirit's as well. We have already spoken of the Father's purpose to transform us into the image of Christ. This is a work of grace but a vital aspect of it is our dwelling in Him. By virtue of union with Him He changes us into His likeness. This is what enables us as God's children to both give and receive the love of God.

> How great is the love the Father has lavished on us. That we should be called the children of God! And that is what we are. 1 John 3:1

His DNA is in us and His presence in us and ours in Him conforms us to His image. The goal is and always has been to bring us into the Fathers' love, a love that is the very essence of who He is. This is the genius of God's plan of salvation. Adam failed, but by uniting Himself with our humanity Christ also united us with His divinity thereby transforming us into the children of God. By becoming like Him we inherit His capacity to love. He succeeds and because we are in Him we share in His victory.

> Now if we are children, then we are heirs - heirs of God and co-heirs with Christ, if indeed we share in His sufferings in order that we may also share in His glory. Romans 8:16

It has ever been the will of our enemy to turn us from the source of this great love, our Lord and Saviour Jesus Christ.

> But I am afraid that just as Eve was deceived by the serpents' cunning your minds may be somehow led astray from your sincere and pure devotion to Christ. 2 Corinthians 11:3

When Jesus speaks those momentous words "I am the way the truth and the life" we rush to apply them to the new birth and then just as quickly move on to the problems of ministry and sustaining our faith in a fallen world while we wait for the consummation of the kingdom. Jesus meant not only was He the beginning (Alpha) and the end (Omega) but that He was the way, the truth and the life for everything in between. It has been the weakness of modern Protestantism to focus on programs, strategies and ministry at the expense of developing intimacy with God. We tend to see value in our devotional life only insomuch as it is a resource for our ministry activity. Worship and contemplation can wait until Heaven. And so we miss the real heart of God, His passion to love us and for us to join Him in a union of loving hearts. Jesus prayed in John 17.

> Father, I want those you have given me to be with me where I am, and to see my glory, the glory you have given me because you loved me before the creation of the world. John 17:24

It was our Lord's passionate desire that we might enter into that very love of the Father. And He is the way to it. We are well acquainted with the judicial work of the cross but weak in both expectation and experience of the relational work of the cross. The Father does not want us to wait for heaven. He wants us to begin now to enter into the joy of loving fellowship with Him. How does that happen? - In and through Jesus. He is still the way. It is in Him that we come to the Father and, as Paul repeatedly stated to the Ephesians, we are in Christ.

> Praise be to the God and Father of our Lord Jesus Christ, who has blessed us in the heavenly realms with <u>every</u> spiritual blessing <u>in Christ</u>. Ephesians 1:3

Jesus is now with the Father and the scriptures tell us we are seated with Him in the heavenlies. (Ephesians 2:6) This is not just judicially true; it is actually true. Of course our minds cannot grasp how Christ can be in us and us in Him, and yet He is in heaven with the Father and we are there with Him at the same time. These are eternal realities but they are the truth and Jesus is not only the way but He is the truth. This is a truth that the enemy has taken advantage of and so deprived many of intimacy with the Father and of a deep personal experience of His love. If it doesn't make sense then it couldn't possibly be true. But for those who have not believed the lie, the greatest discovery of all is there for us to find.

> The kingdom of Heaven is like treasure hidden in a field. When a man found it, he hid it again, and then in his joy went and sold all he had and bought that field. Matthew 13:14

Where is our treasure? It is where our heart is according to our Lord. (Matthew 6:21)

> If we want God to be all in all for us, our heart should

> always be where we will our treasure to be. (Lefebvre)

It is the discovery of the unfailing love of the Father that awaits every child of God and it is this discovery that fills us with a passion to know Him and give all of ourselves to His will and His glory. David knew this from personal experience and so was called a man after God's heart. (Acts 13:22) God said of him "He will do everything I want him to do." David was so in love with God he was utterly committed to the Father's will.

> How priceless is your unfailing love! Both high and low
> among men find refuge in the shadow of your wings.
> (Psalm 36:7)

He had discovered the treasure, the pearl of great price and His heart belonged to God.

The journey to the Father's heart is a journey of faith. It begins with desire and belief in the love of God and then total commitment to digging in your own field to find this priceless treasure.

We leave this ten chapter discourse on walking on the water with the most practical instruction that could be given in a humanly impossible journey. Peter could never have walked on water by himself but somehow he had faith to step out of that boat. As already stated in our introduction, he left no footprints behind for others to follow. The reason for saying this is that this is a personal journey for every individual who undertakes it. God deals with each one of us as unique originals. There is no one like you and there will never be another. You cannot follow anyone else with but one exception. You can follow Jesus who declared that if we kept our eyes on Him we would find our way.

> Let us fix our eyes on Jesus, the author and perfecter of faith, who for the joy set before him endured the cross, scorning its shame, and sat down at the right hand of the throne of God. (Hebrews 12:2)

He began our journey and He is committed to our finishing it. It is our seemingly endless capacity for taking our eyes off of him as Peter did that troubles us. But every time we do we need only cry to Him for help, "Lord, I'm sinking!" And He is ready and full willing to take us by the hand and walk us to safety.

What then will it take for us to enter into the fullness of knowing the Father's love if Jesus is the way, the truth and the life? We are called to strengthen our relationship with Him and so it must be those things that scripture directly connects with knowing Him that we must practice with all we have and are. Jesus stated our greatest call is to love God with <u>all</u> our heart, and soul and strength and mind. There are three disciplines I would commend to you.

The first is obedience. Jesus established a direct connection between obedience and the revelation of the Father's love. John, once again fulfilling his special call as the apostle of love, recorded Jesus' words.

> Whoever has my commands and obeys them, he is the one who loves me. He who loves me will be loved by my Father, and I too will love him and show myself to him.

John 14:21

There is confusion on the question of grace that causes many Christians to disregard this specific cause and effect teaching of our Lord. Since we are saved by grace and that not of ourselves where does obedience enter into our salvation experience. If we focus only on the born again work of grace we can miss the fullness of God's plan. It is a given that God desires to save us from hell but we must remember that the essence of hell's condition is separation from God. We were saved to bring us into a relationship with God and that relationship is to be cultivated and worked on. This is where obedience comes in. God is our Father and as His children we must learn obedience and grow in godliness. Only the Father through the Son and the Spirit can teach us and guide us just as a parent trains and disciplines a child. Underlying this relationship is the love of a father for his child. Jesus makes it clear that our obedience leads to a greater intimacy and experience of the Father's love. Now, this is not a reward based on gaining the Father's approval but a result of being transformed more and more into the image of Christ through hearing and obeying the word of the Father. His purpose is for us to grow and mature and He guides us to that end. As we become more like Christ we find communion with the Father of love more comfortable and natural. Because He is love we must learn to love and become love in our very beings. Thanks be to God this is our inheritance in Christ. There is more to obedience than is often understood. If we need to hear the Father how can we open our spiritual ears to hear what men and women of God have characterized as "the still, small voice."? This brings us to another critical spiritual discipline.

The second discipline is prayer. In fact, we raise a biblical standard for prayer achieved by few and yet commended in scripture:

"Pray without ceasing." 1 Thessalonians 5:17

It is tempting to read this verse and conclude that it is impossible and therefore Paul must be using hyperbole in order to provoke prayer support for his evangelistic mission. But the context indicates that Paul is speaking into the spiritual lives of the Thessalonians. Most Christians find it difficult to maintain a regular morning devotional life that might consist of 15-20 minutes of prayer. It isn't just the discipline aspect of doing so but the experience of running out of things to pray. Praying for any length of time is challenging even when aided by lists of prayer requests. It is the idea of constant intercession that actually defeats and misses the true purpose of prayer. It is a given that we are completely dependent on God. We are needy, weak and fundamentally ignorant of our Lord's eternal kingdom. This tends to focus our prayers in the petition mode and out of touch with prayer as conversation in the context of a relationship.

We have repeatedly pointed out that God's purpose in Christ is to put us into relationship with Himself. As amazing and incomprehensible as it may be to us God actually wants to talk with us and spend time with us. When we think of the call of the Great Commission, there is an aspect of functionality to our prayer life, but even with the call of God on our lives to serve the background of service is relational intimacy with God. It is impossible for us to serve God with any effectiveness apart from deep knowledge of Him as a Person. In short, prayer must be about us getting to know God. Salvation, like marriage, is only a starting point. Imagine a couple going through courtship and a wedding ceremony immediately followed by separation to different cities, their only relationship being through letters and phone calls. Sounds ridiculous but this parallels the spiritual lives of many Christians. In a marriage there is an expectation of intimate union and a lifetime of deepening the relationship through conversation and shared experiences. This is precisely what God seeks with every child of His, a daily ongoing relationship that is sustained by constant prayer. Newlyweds generally want to spend as much time as possible together. This should be the heart of every child of God, especially as we have the privilege of getting to know the greatest Person in the universe.

How do we do this? We talk to Him about everything as though the Lord Jesus was Himself by our side every moment of our day. The truth is, that is exactly where He is. The God who sees the sparrow fall to the ground and who has numbered the very hairs on our heads is intimately involved with the minutest details of our lives. He cares about all of it and expects us to share all of it with Him. In the beginning this is difficult but if we persist it becomes a habit. There are some useful things that can be done to develop a continual prayer life.

Pray through the Psalms. They are a record of David's relationship with God. He evidently had a life of continual prayer and a deep intimacy with God. The Psalms record his responses to almost every situation that could be imagined and they give us a sense of how we can talk to God.

David said he prayed 3 times/day (Psalm 55:17), but praised 7 times/day (Psalm 119:164). There is abundant scriptural support for the practice of the seven "hours" of prayer. Peter and John went to the temple in Acts 3 'at the third hour' of prayer. It may seem unrealistic to do this in the context of a busy life unless we look at these times as a brief turning to the Lord. Don't over think or over do but there is no reason why we cannot take a few minutes at noon, when we come home from work, before we sleep at night or even during work breaks. The point is to practice continually turning to God, to bring Him into everything we do, to end our unconscious division between the sacred and the secular. Our notions of sacred places and times actually dishonor the infinite, omnipresent God we worship. This can gradually become normal as we pray about everything we face during our daily routine. God wants us to share all of our life with Him. It is up to us to let Him in. The third discipline is the most difficult. The scriptures speak of it as "waiting on the Lord." We have a tremendous drive to do, to be busy in western culture. In fact we are uncomfortable with silence and inactivity. If we are not working we are on the Internet, watching TV or listening to music on IPods. We can't even go to a restaurant or shop in a department store without background music. Silence is a rare commodity and it is becoming rarely sought for except when we want to sleep. Waiting on God is a listening experience best practiced in silence. It is a time when we seek to hear God speak or to simply contemplate His presence. The first scriptural reference to this is in Genesis 24:63.

> "He (Isaac) went out to the field one evening to meditate…"

The word for meditate is our best understanding of the Hebrew phrase 'turn one's face toward God'. The translators select meditate in an attempt to put some activity into what Isaac is doing but they miss the true meaning. "Contemplate" might have been a better choice but the reality is that Isaac went out to listen to God. He went out to a place of quiet away from any interference or disturbance so he could hear what God might say. This practice is the lifeline of every child of God who comes to know Him and effectively serve Him. Prayer is not so much bringing our perspective to God as it is discovering and receiving His. It is certain He knows everything and just as surely we have a very limited perspective. It makes little sense for us to tell God what we think He should do when we can hear directly from Him His will and purpose. This kind of intimacy with God is rare for the simple reason that few know it is available and fewer still are willing to seek it out.

In earlier chapters we have talked of many aspects of our relationship with God. They all come down to this question of knowing Him, something that can only happen on His terms. When we speak of prayer we are not so much concerned, as many books on prayer are, with how to get answers but with how to get to know God. We are in fact speaking of a love affair with God Himself. David put it succinctly.

> One thing I ask of the Lord, this is what I seek: that I may dwell in the house of the Lord all the days of my life, to gaze upon the beauty of the Lord and to seek Him in His temple. Psalm 27:14

David was saying that if he could have what he really wanted it would be to spend all of his time seeking the Lord and beholding His face. David was a king and his duties surely made this impossible but this was his heart and the Psalms indicate that he gave every available moment to worship and prayer including the night watches.
It is hard for us to imagine this unless we consider this relationship with the One who is love the Pearl of Great Price for which we are willing to exchange everything. Are we willing to so passionately seek Him that we will give up everything that distracts us from it – the distractions of a world that will soon pass away and leave us with nothing of value but our relationship with God. The beauty of this is that this is what He wants for every one of His children – to love them so that they know they are loved. This is what He created us for and God does not expect us to wait

for heaven to enjoy it. God is love and He would do no less than love us with a love that is unfailing. God is looking for lovers, those who have the determination of David. Only "one thing" matters to them – knowing God.

Conclusion

A.W. Tozer had a gift for pithy sayings that touch the heart in the most vulnerable places, places we would rather hide and protect from any outward intrusion or exposure.

> You can be as straight as a gun barrel theologically and as empty as one spiritually.[14]

Ours is a generation and a time of theology without experience. The vast majority of those who profess Christ know little of intimacy with God and might even be accused of "having a form of godliness but denying the power thereof." (2 Corinthians 3:5) I have spoken of ignorance as a factor. One of the unfortunate by-products of the reformation was a disconnect with the traditions of mysticism that can be traced back to the early church. Protestants assumed that anything taught by Catholic priests was suspect and thus untrustworthy. As a consequence we lost the teachings of great men of God who served as spiritual guides to the deeper life that leads to union with God and the true meaning of prayer – Fenelon, Molinos, Hilton, John of the Cross, Bernard of Clairvaux, de Sales, the Desert Fathers, to name a few. In our rush to straighten the gun barrel theologically as we rightfully saw the deficiencies of Catholicism at the time, we ran the risk of becoming empty spiritually. The emphasis on right doctrine endangered the call to right relationship. Lack of teaching is a fair excuse but we Protestants must allow that we have had greater access to the Word of God in the last 400 years than at any other time in church history. Do we indeed have an excuse based on ignorance or is there

---

[14] Tozer, Tozer Speaks.

another reality that has kept us from the deeper life? To this Tozer speaks once again.

> "We settle for words in religion because deeds are too costly." [15]

The price of intimacy with God is high. In fact the price is all we have and all we are. Jesus laid down His life to purchase ours by His blood, not just a part but the whole. Every child of God knows this because this is the witness of the Spirit of God in us. Knowing the outstanding death warrant on our self-life our instinct is to flee or, as Adam and Eve did, hide behind the bushes of doctrinal fidelity and orthodoxy. We were made to be filled with all the fullness of Christ and to know the love of God that passes understanding. And yet there is a fear in us that approaches terror of the cost that we must pay.

We have spoken of this in the chapter on the end of self and also of the role of grace but we must never forget that what God asks of us is an exchange – our life for His. He offers us all of Himself in exchange for all of our self-life, our weakness for His strength, our selfishness for His love, our sadness for His joy, our anxiety for His peace and our death for His life. What we give is nothing in comparison with what we receive.

The purpose of a life of prayer and the pursuit of God is this exchange, one we desperately need, for apart from it we are unable to enter into the fullness of fellowship with God, which is our destiny for all eternity, that for which we were created.

---

[15] Tozer, ibid.

The teachings in each of the chapters of this book are meant to guide you in your pursuit of God. It is the most difficult journey possible as illustrated by the metaphor we began with. It is exactly akin to walking on water. But we know it can be done because Jesus did it first and He bids you as He did Peter to step out of the boat and come. Like Peter you will certainly falter but all you need do is cry for help and the Lord will bear you up. Prayer, at its most honest, is a cry for help.

But the Lord does want you to walk on water. With this knowledge you can begin to pursue Him with full assurance that if you seek Him with all your heart you will find Him.

> "To know God is to step out of time into eternity, to find oneself in a vast ocean of love with no shores."[16]
>
> "God's love for us answers all of our questions."[17]
>
> "The road which leads to God is as hidden and secret from the soul as is a road across water from the eyes. Tracks and footprints make no mark on it; likewise the signs of God in the souls He draws towards Him by making them grow in wisdom are also as a rule unseen."[18]

---

[16] Peter Hay, Journal, 2011.

[17] Lefebvre, Simplicity, 64.

[18] St, John of the Cross, The Dark Night of the Soul, Bk. 11, Chapter 17.